THE
MENTOR'S
GUIDE

THE MENTOR'S GUIDE

*Facilitating Effective
Learning Relationships*

Lois J. Zachary

Foreword by Laurent A. Daloz

JOSSEY-BASS
A Wiley Company
San Francisco

FLIP

Jossey-Bass books and products are available through most bookstores. To contact Jossey-Bass directly, call (888) 378-2537, fax to (800) 605-2665, or visit our website at www.josseybass.com.
Substantial discounts on bulk quantities of Jossey-Bass books are available to corporations, professional associations, and other organizations. For details and discount information, contact the special sales department at Jossey-Bass.

Library of Congress Cataloging-in-Publication Data
Zachary, Lois J.
  The mentor's guide : facilitating effective learning relationships /
Lois J. Zachary ; foreword by Laurent Daloz.— 1st ed.
     p. cm. — (The Jossey-Bass higher and adult education series)
Includes bibliographical references (p.   ).
    ISBN 0-7879-4742-3 (alk. paper)
  1. Mentoring in education. 2. Learning, Psychology of. 3.
Interpersonal relations. I. Title. II. Series.
    LB1731.4 .Z23 2000
    371.102—dc21   00-008194

FIRST EDITION
PB Printing   10 9 8 7 6 5 4 3 2 1

The Jossey-Bass
Higher and Adult Education Series

Contents

A friend of mine sent me a drawing by artist Brian Andreas with a quote sketched into it. It reads, "Most people don't know that there are angels whose only job is to make sure you don't get too comfortable and fall asleep and miss your life."

Its words resonate in my ears as I write this dedication to my "angels," Ed, Bruce, and Lisa who I can always count on to make sure I don't get too comfortable, fall asleep, and miss my life.

L.J.Z.

Foreword

Ecologists tell us that a tree planted in a clearing of an old forest will grow more successfully than one planted in an open field. The reason, it seems, is that the roots of the forest tree are able to follow the intricate pathways created by former trees and thus embed themselves more deeply. Indeed, over time, the roots of many trees may actually graft themselves to one another, creating an interdependent mat of life hidden beneath the earth. This literally enables the stronger trees to share resources with the weaker so the whole forest becomes healthier.

Similarly, human beings thrive best when we grow in the presence of those who have gone before. Our roots may not follow every available pathway, but we are able to become more fully ourselves because of the presence of others. "I am who I am because we are," goes the saying, and mentors are a vital part of the often invisible mat of our lives.

There have, of course, always been mentors, but our ability to name them as such is relatively recent. Psychologists discovered them only a generation ago; educators and the business world were not far behind. Since then, mentors have become a hot item, appearing in best sellers, television specials, and on film. Generally they are viewed as people who help us find a jewel of wisdom or a promotion at work. Ultimately, however, mentors are more than that. As Zalman Schachter-Shalomi says, they "impart lessons in the art of living." Great mentors extend the human activity of care beyond the bounds of the family. They see us in ways that we have not been seen before. And at their best they inspire us to reach beyond ourselves; they show us how to make a positive difference in a wider world.

Lois Zachary knows a lot about that. Coming from a background in human development, she has had years of direct experience in organizational change, leadership education, and mentoring. In this book, she brings her experience together with an impressive range of resources to create a trove of practical knowledge and concrete exercises for all of us who seek to serve as mentors in more adequate and humane ways. True to the essence of mentoring, the activities here are artfully designed not to preach about one "right way" to be a mentor but rather to help the reader to see his or her own mentoring style and preferences more clearly and thus, to learn from direct experience and observation.

Zachary knows that good mentoring is tough, and she peppers her numerous examples with instances of inadequate or failed mentoring. The journey of mentor and mentee runs along narrow and daunting ledges as well as high outlooks and is not for the fainthearted or indifferent. She bluntly warns of dangers along the way even while offering priceless assistance in the form of savvy observations and solid advice. The section on feedback alone is worth the price of the book, as is the annotated bibliography.

Moving beyond the superficiality and formulas that too often mark the literature on mentoring, Zachary reminds us that it is the particularity of each relationship that really matters, that human development always takes place in a larger context that mentors ignore at their peril. Moreover, the exercises here invite us to explore more profoundly our own capacities for establishing genuine trust with others, for listening with real respect and compassion, for examining clear-eyed our own inflations and convenient delusions. Again and again, she reminds us that the central "skill" of an effective mentor is no less than the capacity for self-awareness—a willingness to keep a relentless, if forgiving, eye on our own journey as well as that of our companion.

There is much here for all of us to learn from. One of the speakers in the book plaintively remarks that what she really needs is "a mentor to mentor me about mentoring." With *The Mentor's Guide*, Lois Zachary has stepped forward to start us on our way toward becoming more adept in this vital, nourishing, and profoundly human role as we open the way for those coming after us to sink their roots deeper, to grow fuller, and to participate more richly in the interdependent mat of life.

January 2000   LAURENT A. PARKS DALOZ
Clinton, Washington

Preface

Good intention is not enough to facilitate effective learning in a mentoring relationship. Mentors who become students of their own experience use reflection to inform what it is they do and how they do it. In reflecting on their experience, they learn something about themselves and as a result are better prepared to facilitate effective learning relationships. They become reflective practitioners (Schön, 1983), modeling the self-directed learning they seek to promote in others.

When the mentoring experience is consciously and conscientiously grounded in learning, the likelihood that the mentoring relationship will become a satisfactory learning relationship for both mentoring partners dramatically improves.

The assortment of reasons that people choose to become mentors are legion. Some desire to repay a debt to society. ("So many have given to me," they think. "Now it is my turn to give back to those who will come after me.") Some do it because they are asked. Some feel an obligation to support the next generation of chief executive officers, researchers, or community or organizational leaders. Mentoring is the way some organizations do business ("Everyone who works here is expected to be a mentor or a mentee."). And some see it as a calling ("I felt that mentoring was something I could be doing to be a better contributor.").

Over the years, the objective of the mentoring relationship has evolved from the mentee's learning to an approach rooted in principles of adult learning. This learner-centered shift in the approach to mentoring requires that a mentor facilitate the learning relationship rather than transfer knowledge to the learner. According to Stephen Brookfield (1986), effective facilitation is characterized by the conditions of voluntary engagement of both partners, mutual respect for the mentee's individuality, collaboration, critical reflection, and empowerment of the learner.

Facilitating Effective Learning Relationships

This book focuses on the mentor's key tasks and processes for enhancing learning rather than on projected time frames and psychological milestones. Successful completion of these tasks and facilitative processes makes it possible for each partner to move in, move through, and move on in their learning relationship (Schlossberg, Lynch, and Chickering, 1989). These predictable phases are present in formal and informal mentoring relationships, whether one is aware of them or not. When they are disregarded, they can have a negative impact on a relationship.

Effective mentoring relationships begin with preparation of the mentor and move onto preparation of the relationship. The next stage is negotiation of the relationship—that is, the conversation that results in a mutual understanding of the process that the mentoring relationship is to follow. This conversation becomes the road map for the relationship. The third phase is the longest and presents the greatest challenge for both mentee and mentor. This is the enabling phase, when there is the most need for learner support. Coming to closure, the fourth phase, is a continuation of the process that began the moment the learning goals were articulated. It continues until the goals are achieved and a decision is made to end or renegotiate the relationship. Coming to closure is the most neglected of the four phases. By letting a mentoring relationship fade out like the sunset, an opportunity for learning is missed.

In preparing for a mentoring relationship, mentors do not usually consider what is required to move on to the next phase. However, knowledge about the phases greatly contributes to creating a solid understanding of the learning that occurs in the mentoring relationship.

Despite the number of books on mentoring, there are few resources that provide process tools, strategies, and techniques for understanding and operationalizing the mentoring process. This book is a practical guide that lays out the processes from beginning to end and provides tools for creating an effective learning relationship. The focal point is the learning relationship and the people in it.

Who Should Read This Book

This book can be used by readers in the business world and by those working in nonprofit and higher education settings. The examples used in this book are all drawn from actual mentoring experiences in a variety of situations. This book will be of value to those who are in (or about to begin) mentoring relationships, as well as to those who wish to learn about mentoring. It can be used as a self-help book, a compendium of resources for helping to facilitate mentee learning, an introduction to mentoring for first-time mentors, or an opportunity for seasoned mentors. And although *The Mentor's Guide* provides serious guidance for individuals, *serious* is not to be confused with *formal*.

The Mentor's Guide offers a framework for informed mentoring practice. It provides insight into the nature and focus on the process of mentoring, so that the learning of the mentor can be facilitated in ways that enrich, enable, enliven, and engage the learning of the mentee. It describes a variety of interactive opportunities to explore issues and concepts in depth and provides an array of practical tips for achieving a productive and effective mentoring partnership.

For some readers, *The Mentor's Guide* may be the extent of their mentoring preparation. For others, this book will complement mentoring training and coaching programs. It is not designed to be a comprehensive reference about everything there is to know about mentoring. Rather, it presents an array of practical options, steps, and strategies for action and reflection and is useful in a variety of settings to help facilitate the mentee's learning.

Not all mentoring arises from an institutional base, however. In fact, most mentoring relationships do not. Because this book concentrates on facilitating learning relationships, it can be used by an individual mentor independently of organizational affiliation or by community groups. Its perspective has no institutional walls.

How to Use This Book

The Mentor's Guide draws on Larry Daloz's *Effective Teaching and Mentoring* (1986), recently in a second edition as *Mentor: Guiding the Journey of Adult Learners* (1999). It can be used as a companion to it or as a stand-alone guide. Daloz's learner-centered focus is compelling. By intimately focusing on the learner and the learning connection and the learning process, Daloz reaches into the very core of mentoring.

The Mentor's Guide combines discussion and workbook-like elements to support those who are in the process of facilitating learning in mentoring relationships. It does not matter if the relationship is formal or informal or whether a mentor has identified a mentee or the mentee has recruited the mentor. These exercises and reflections can be used by mentors to prepare for mentoring sessions. They can be used as is or modified. The exhibits and exercises can be used as discussion points for mentoring conversations. These resources are helpful reminders to keep the focus on the learning and the learners.

This book articulates a definite set of assumptions about the nature of mentoring work:

- Mentoring can be a powerful growth experience for both the mentor and the mentee. Mentors will learn new things about their mentee, themselves, and their organizations (if this relationship is in an organizational context).

- Mentoring is a process of engagement. No one can mentor without connection. In fact, mentoring is most successful when it is done collaboratively. Commitment by and engagement of mentoring partners is a key element in establishing, maintaining, and experiencing successful mentoring relationships.

- Facilitating successful mentoring is a reflective practice that takes preparation and dedication. It begins with self-learning. Taking the time to prepare for the relationship adds value to it.

- Mentoring with staying power focuses on the learners, the learning process, and the learning. *The Mentor's Guide* models that approach by providing exhibits and exercises to stimulate more informed mentoring practice.

Where adults find themselves in the present moment becomes a starting point for learning (Lindeman, 1989). As you read this book, there are several approaches you might follow:

Start with your questions. Use this book as a reference when you have a question. Frame your question first, and consult the index for where you might find the answer.

Start at the beginning. Proceed step by step and work your way through the entire book from start to finish. Complete the exercises in logical sequence.

Start at the Contents. Scan the Contents page. Consider the topics that interest you, and start with those.

Start with the stumbling blocks. Identify what is getting in the way of your mentoring relationship. What do you need help with first?

Start where you are right now. Locate yourself in relation to the four phases of the mentoring relationship: at the beginning (preparing, negotiating), the middle (enabling), or near the end (coming to closure). Use the checklists provided in the exercises at the end of Chapters Four through Seven to determine your readiness to move on to the next phase.

Start with your learning style. We all learn in different ways. In this book, what at first may appear to be duplication is intentional. Some exercises will mesh with your style and situation; others will not. Some will be more appropriate for one-to-one mentoring; others will work better in group settings. Choose what is appropriate to your style, your way of learning, and your needs.

You may need time to reflect before taking action. A broad perspective and exercises for critical reflection may have particular appeal to you. Or you may be an information seeker and gatherer and learn best by reading about lots of different options and approaches. If you prefer to focus on the concrete and practical, you may find yourself experimenting with a variety of the options presented. The sentence stems that appear throughout *The Mentor's Guide* might be just what you need to get focused on a particular content area. All you might need is a trigger to stimulate your thinking. If you prefer hands-on experience, you might be more likely to work through the exercises yourself, as well as with your mentee.

Overview of Chapters

Chapter One is solidly embedded in learning as a way to frame the mentor's work. Using experience as a lens, mentors observe their own developmental journey, explore the concept of personal ecology in learning, get a better grasp on the concept of facilitation, and gain some perspective about the concept of learning styles.

Chapter Two focuses on the context of the learning—that is, the environment or climate within which the relationship grows and is supported. It includes setting, location, situation, culture, and circumstances. Context presents special challenges in mentoring relationships, particularly in promoting long-distance and cross-cultural learning.

Chapter Three presents an overview of each of four mentoring relationship phases and discusses themes that run throughout the phases, along with related tools and techniques.

Chapters Four through Seven provide an in-depth look at each of the phases of a mentoring relationship. Chapter Four offers strategies for mentor self-preparation, including an exploration of motivation and a mentoring skills inventory. The focus then shifts to establishing mentor learning priorities, developing goals, creating a mentoring development action plan, and exploring role definitions. The second part of the chapter zeroes in on preparing the relationship, with strategies for engaging the mentee, identifying assumptions, and preparing for initial mentoring conversations.

Chapter Five describes seven mentoring negotiation outcomes: well-defined goals, success criteria and measurement, delineation of mutual responsibility, accountability, protocols for addressing stumbling blocks, consensual mentoring agreement, and a work plan for achieving learning goals. These outcomes form the basis for developing, crafting, and executing a viable mentoring agreement.

Chapter Six looks at the enabling phase, where mentoring partners spend the most time, where dangers lurk, and where the work of the relationship is accomplished and the opportunity for the greatest growth and most frequent derailment exists. Enabling involves putting the concepts of support, challenge, and vision to work. It means creating a learning environment, building and maintaining the relationship, monitoring and evaluating the process, fostering reflection, and assessing learning outcomes. Engaging in meaningful feedback and overcoming obstacles are explored specifically as they apply to the enabling phase of the relationship.

Coming to closure is an evolutionary process. Recognizing the need for closure rests on being alert to signals, which may indicate that it is time for closure. Chapter Seven offers strategies for achieving meaningful closure. The key is reaching a learning conclusion so that learning is elevated to the next level of application and integration.

A mentor's work of nurturing growth in others sometimes leaves little room for time to be reflective about one's own growth. Chapter Eight frames the discussion of personal development for the mentor through an exploration of reflection, renewal, and regeneration.

Appendix A presents tools and guidelines for those who administer and supervise mentoring programs. This appendix complements preexisting programs by stimulating thoughtful reflection (and learning) about how to create, build, and improve a program. Appendix B contains an array of resources for specific areas of need or interest. The resources are organized by chapter topic and can be used as references in exploring specific aspects of mentoring relationships.

The Mentor as Facilitator

Today's mentor is a facilitative partner in an evolving learning relationship focused on meeting mentee learning goals and objectives. In order to maximize that relationship, mentors too must grow and develop. Facilitating a learning relationship starts with self-learning. Without a mentor's commitment to personal learning, the potential effectiveness of the learning relationship is greatly reduced.

As you read and use the materials in this book, "reach out, keep reaching out, keep bringing in" (Piercy, 1982, p. 128). It will enable you to reap an enduring harvest.

March 2000   LOIS J. ZACHARY
Phoenix, Arizona

Acknowledgments

When I began writing *The Mentor's Guide,* I never could have imagined that so many people would play such a significant role in bringing it to fruition. Many friends, colleagues, clients, and family members contributed with encouragement, stories, questions, feedback, and patient understanding. Their contributions were made with care and consideration, and they matter very much to me. These individuals have enriched the writing experience and pushed me to a much deeper place in my thinking and my practice.

I extend my heartfelt thanks to the following people:

My colleagues Barbara Vinear, Lorrie Appleton, Peggy Boyle, Gloria Sandvik, Connie Wolf, Amy Webb, Marilyn Oyler, and Lee Herman, who with their gentle yet firm prodding, poking, and candor honored me with the gift of feedback.

My client, student, and friend Margaret Hamstead, for her help.

My editor at Jossey-Bass, Gale Erlandson, and Rachel Livsey, development editor, for their inspiration and wisdom.

Stephen Brookfield and Larry Daloz, luminaries in the field of adult learning, for their profound influence on my work and my thinking.

The Author

Lois J. Zachary, a specialist in adult development and learning, is the principal of Leadership Development Services, a consulting firm located in Phoenix, Arizona, that offers leadership coaching, education, and training for corporate and not-for-profit organizations across the continent. She is a program associate of Leadership Center West, based in San Jose, California, which focuses on achieving organizational effectiveness by improving the quality of people's lives at work.

Zachary's workshops, keynotes, consultations, and retreats integrate adult development and learning theory with methods to improve leadership development and organizational effectiveness. She coaches leaders and their organizations in designing, implementing, and evaluating learner-centered mentoring programs. She is a 1998 recipient of the Athena Award in Recognition of Excellence in Mentoring for her research in mentoring.

She is a national lecturer for Programs for Higher Education, a doctoral program of Nova Southeastern University. She is also a certified Myers-Briggs trainer.

Zachary's publications include articles, monographs, and books about adult development and learning, mentoring, leadership and board development, staff development, adult Jewish learning, and the basics of establishing and maintaining a consulting practice. Her column, "Board Room," appears regularly in *Arizona Corridors Magazine*.

THE
MENTOR'S
GUIDE

CHAPTER 1

Grounding the Work

Focusing on Learning

If you tend them properly, if you mulch, if you water,
if you provide birds that eat insects a home and winter food,
if the sun shines and you pick off caterpillars,
if the praying mantis comes and the ladybugs and the bees,
then the plants flourish, but at their own internal clock.
—MARGE PIERCY, "The Seven of Pentacles"

Learning is the fundamental process and the primary purpose of mentoring. One of the principal reasons that mentoring relationships fail is that the learning process is not tended to and the focus on learning goals is not maintained.

This chapter grounds the mentor's work in a learner-centered approach to mentoring. It presents a mentoring paradigm consistent with andragogical principles (Knowles, 1980) and congruent with best practices of adult learning.

The role of experience is a primary force in understanding the parallel journeys of the mentor and mentee and the learning relationship. It is grounded in a web of connection and interrelationship that is explored through the vehicle of personal ecology—forces that affect how we learn. The notions of challenge, support, and vision along with learning style play a critical role in facilitating the learning process.

Maintaining the Focus on Learning

"Tending properly" (Piercy, 1982) helps to maintain the focus on the mentee's learning goals yet is one of the biggest challenges in the mentor's work. When learning is not tended to, the mentoring process is reduced to a transaction, the integrity of the learning is compromised, and the relationship is undermined. Consider what happened to Randy and Pat.

Randy, a manager in a multinational corporation, had been assigned as Pat's mentor. Pat, a new employee, was bright, energetic, highly motivated, and eager to make a mark. Their relationship started out on a mutually positive note, and they developed rapport easily. But shortly into their relationship, the level of interaction dramatically shifted. Anxious to please this high-level executive, Pat willingly carried Randy's briefcase, worked on his projects, and researched whatever topics Randy assigned. As time progressed, Randy's responsibilities increased, and Randy and Pat saw each other less and less. Before long, the quality of their interaction shifted from two-way information sharing and discussion to transaction and information giving, and their exchanges became increasingly intermittent. There was little, if any, discussion of the learning taking place and no time available for raising or answering questions. Even their e-mail exchanges were brusque.

What was missing was an opportunity to discuss and process the learning that was taking place. Pat was a quick learner and learned a lot by shadowing Randy (that is, observing Randy in action). Yet the learning was not very satisfactory.

Jocelyn, too, had high ambitions for herself and realized that there were specific skills that she needed in order to get ahead. She approached Carmon, a high performer and much-admired manager in her organization, to be her mentor. At the first meeting Carmon worked with Jocelyn in crystallizing her somewhat amorphous learning goals. They agreed that it was Jocelyn's responsibility to initiate the contact between them.

Each time they met, Carmon and Jocelyn reviewed the progress they were making against Jocelyn's learning goals. They also set aside regular time to talk about their level of satisfaction with the relationship and how each felt things were going. There was one potential rough spot they had to work through: Jocelyn wanted to move faster and make a claim on more of Carmon's time. Because they had intentionally built reflection time into their regular meetings, they were able to talk about Jocelyn's concerns and identify other venues for learning, including several projects, client meetings, and strategic internal meetings.

The Learner-Centered Mentoring Paradigm

The two examples illustrate the difference that tending to the learning and the learning process can make in a mentoring relationship. Randy and Pat's subservient mentoring relationship is not unique to the corporate world; there are similar examples in academia where the mentee is so eager to get ahead that the exposure that comes with "carrying a professor's briefcase" makes the experience worthwhile. Jocelyn also had high ambitions, but her relationship with Carmon reflected a more collaborative learning partnership.

The phrase *learning partnership* is congruent with the learner-centered mentoring paradigm, which is grounded in knowledge about adult learning. The learner—in this case the mentee—plays a more active role in the learning than in the former mentor-driven paradigm, even when the mentee has been recruited by the mentor. The mentor's role has been replaced from the "sage on the stage" to the "guide on the side." There has been a shift away from the more traditional authoritarian teacher–dependent student–supplicant paradigm, where the passive mentee sits at the feet of the master and receives knowledge. Today, "wisdom is not passed from an authoritarian teacher to a supplicant student, but is discovered in a learning relationship in which both stand to gain a greater understanding of the workplace and the world" (Aubrey and Cohen, 1995, p. 161). The mentor is now less authority figure and more facilitator. The more the mentor is engaged in facilitating the learning relationship, the more the facilitator engages the mentee in the learning process by creating a climate conducive to learning.

Instead of being mentor driven, with the mentor taking full responsibility for the mentee's learning, the mentee learns to share responsibility for the learning setting, priorities, learning, and resources and becomes increasingly self-directed. When the learner is not ready to assume that degree of responsibility, the mentor nurtures and develops the mentee's capacity for self-direction (from dependence to independence to interdependence) over the course of the relationship. As the learning relationship evolves, the mentoring partners share the accountability and responsibility for achieving a mentee's learning goals.

It used to be that the length of mentoring relationship continued for a period of years. Generally today's mentoring relationships span a shorter time period, with duration tied to the accomplishment of specific learning goals rather than broad, diffuse goals. When mentoring relationships continue beyond that period of time, the mentoring partners revisit, recast, and renegotiate the goals.

The model of "a mentor for all seasons and all reasons" is an unrealistic expectation that lays an exhausting burden of expectation on a mentor. A more desirable situation for a mentee is to have multiple mentors over a lifetime, and even at the same time. A recent study commissioned by Deloitte & Touche and the Corporate State found that almost three-quarters of the Generation X-ers they interviewed like the idea of having several mentors with varying levels of expertise (Rodgers, 1999).

There are many models and opportunities available for mentoring. Some institutions run mentoring groups or mentoring circles, where mentors facilitate the learning of a group of individuals. In peer mentoring groups and pairs (sometimes called reverse mentoring), individuals mentor each other, and intact business mentoring teams help fledgling businesses. In the mentoring personal board of directors model, an individual identifies a variety of goals and learning objectives and then recruits individual mentors (the "board of directors") to help him or her achieve the desired goals. Each "board member" mentors the individual to achieve specific desired outcomes.

It used to be that learning was set in primarily face-to-face interaction, with correspondence or telephone conversation used to supplement that contact. Today technology has extended the opportunity for contact, and long-distance mentoring is much more common than in the past. Multiple and varied venues and opportunities often supplement face-to-face mentoring sessions. For example, a mentee might meet in person with a mentor to discuss goals. The next step could be a chatroom meeting on-line or e-mail exchange to refine and focus the goals. The mentee might shadow the mentor or work on a project related to learning goals.

The focus of the mentoring has also shifted. It has moved from a product-oriented model, characterized by the transfer of knowledge, to a process-oriented relationship involving knowledge acquisition, application, and critical reflection.

The shift in best mentoring practice is consistent with what we know about adult learning (Knowles, 1980):

- Adults learn best when they are involved in diagnosing, planning, implementing, and evaluating their own learning.

- The role of the facilitator is to create and maintain a supportive climate that promotes conditions necessary for learning to take place.

- Adult learners have a need to be self-directing.

- Readiness for learning increases when there is a specific need to know.

- Life's reservoir of experience is a primary learning resource; the life experiences of others enrich the learning process.

- Adult learners have an inherent need for immediacy of application.

- Adults respond best to learning when they are internally motivated to learn.

The elements of the learner-centered mentoring paradigm are set out in Exhibit 1.1.

The Role of Experience

"Everything that happens to you is your teacher," writes Polly Berends (1990). "The secret is to learn to sit at the feet of your own life and be taught by it." When mentors do not take the time to "sit at the feet of their own experience," they bypass significant opportunities for learning. It is beneficial to look at experiences from multiple vantage points. These perspectives help us see more clearly, reach deeper levels of understanding, and ultimately maximize what we learn from them.

A story told about Louis Agassiz, a natural history professor at Harvard University, and his student over a century ago (Corey, 1980) underscores the importance of reflecting on experience to reach deeper levels of understanding.

Agassiz assigned his student the task of observing a fish and left him alone. The student, bored with the assigned work, concluded after a short while that he had "seen all there is to see." To fill his time while waiting for Professor Agassiz to return, he took a pencil and paper and drew the fish. And as he drew, he discovered features he had not previously observed. When the professor returned, the student eagerly reported what he had found from observing and drawing the fish. Although Agassiz at first praised his student and remarked, "A pencil is one of the best of eyes," he later challenged him, saying, "You have not looked very carefully! Why you haven't even seen one of the most conspicuous features of the animal, which is as plainly before your eyes as the fish itself. Look again, look again."

This scene between Agassiz and his student repeated itself over and over again. And with each new observation by the student, Agassiz offered a compliment, followed by a challenge to "look, look again."

There are many lessons to be learned from this classic story. For example, rather than telling the student the answer, Agassiz provided an oppor-

EXHIBIT 1.1

Elements in the Learner-Centered Mentoring Paradigm

Mentoring Element	Changing Paradigm	Adult Learning Principle
Mentee role	From: Passive receiver To: Active partner	Adults learn best when they are involved in diagnosing, planning, implementing, and evaluating their own learning.
Mentor role	From: Authority To: Facilitator	The role of the facilitator is to create and maintain a supportive climate that promotes the conditions necessary for learning to take place.
Learning process	From: Mentor directed and responsible for mentee's learning To: Self-directed and mentee responsible for own learning	Adult learners have a need to be self-directing.
Length of relationship	From: Calendar focus To: Goal determined	Readiness for learning increases when there is a specific need to know.
Mentoring relationship	From: One life = one mentor; one mentor = one mentee To: Multiple mentors over a lifetime and multiple models for mentoring: individual, group, peer models	Life's reservoir of experience is a primary learning resource; the life experiences of others add enrichment to the learning process.
Setting	From: Face-to-face To: Multiple and varied venues and opportunities	Adult learners have an inherent need for immediacy of application.
Focus	From: Product oriented: knowledge transfer and acquisition To: Process oriented: Critical reflection and application	Adults respond best to learning when they are internally motivated to learn.

tunity for self-discovery and reflection. In addition, he paced the learning to be sensitive to the student's need and continuously encouraged him to examine the fish from many different perspectives and look more deeply.

The tools presented throughout this book offer opportunity and challenge to "look, look again" and learn from experience. Mentors who use that learning to full advantage in mentoring relationships are better prepared to enhance the learning of a mentee. They are also better prepared to encourage the mentee to learn from their experiences.

The Mentor's Journey

In order to lay a solid foundation for building an effective learning relationship, mentors must have a clear understanding of their own personal journey. Mentors who fail to differentiate between self and other in a mentoring relationship run the risk of mentor cloning, that is, projecting their own lived experience onto the mentee. The result is that the mentee learning tends to be formulaic, learning is not individualized, and the mentee ends up front and center on the mentor's stage rather than on his or her own.

The journey metaphor captures the meandering quality of the movement that follows us throughout life as we face new challenges. Each challenge itself forms a journey of its own. Along the journey, we experience unexpected delights, lurking dangers, doors opening and closing, change, and ennui.

Observing the Journey

> In the mentoring process, reflection enables us to slow down, rest, and observe our journey and the process of self-knowledge that is so important along the way (Huang and Lynch, 1995, p. 57).

There are three steps in the journey observation process. The first step is self-awareness, which is triggered by self-reflection; it is fundamental to understanding the mentor's proper role in facilitating effective learning relationships.

The second step is to understand the mentee's journey. Mentees bring their own history of experience to a mentoring relationship. Rather than assume what that history and experience is, a mentor who engages the mentee in a discussion of that experience can better avoid the mentor cloning trap.

The third step is to gain perspective, for mentors to look again at their journey and that of the mentee(s). What mentors learn from observing these separate and distinct paths has direct implications for the learning out-comes.

The Journey Time Line

Mentors are an amalgamation of their life experiences and need to be aware of the major events that have influenced them. By becoming a student of their own journey, mentors are better able to understand its flow and pattern. It is also a telling way to test out assumptions. A healthy sense of perspective is useful in guiding a mentee's learning journey.

There are many ways to depict a journey. The way you choose will be uniquely your own. You may choose to construct a journey time line using a word processor, making notes, or using a tape recorder. You may prefer a more pictorial or graphic approach. The means for completion are not as important as taking the time to reflect on your personal journey and to consider the movement that has brought you to the place you are at right now in your life.

Miriam   Miriam had volunteered to be a mentor to women who were looking to make a transition in their careers. In preparing for her role as mentor, she constructed a time line of her own journey.

A utility company had hired Miriam immediately after she completed her associate degree at the local community college. After ten years in a variety of positions, she was promoted to a managerial position. A number of years later, her daughter was fatally injured in a hit-and-run accident. Not long after, she decided to pursue a nursing degree, which she did three years later. She left the company to take a job as floor nurse at a local hospital and now holds a managerial position at the hospital.

In constructing a time line of her journey from line worker to nursing director, Miriam identified the following significant life events as having shaped her development: two marriages, a divorce, the death of her daughter, going back to school, specific job promotions, and a fortieth birthday celebration. Three specific opportunities helped her grow and develop: a mentoring relationship with a woman who was "a fabulous role model for the possible," the educational opportunity provided by the company, and a spouse who was her "cheerleader, guide, and support." But many experiences also blocked her development along the way: living with a spouse who could not understand her dreams and ambitions, tedious work, and coworkers who tried to undermine her educational advancement.

She would be the first to say that there were serendipitous events and experiences that contributed to her growth and development. One of these was meeting Charlotte, her mentor, at a neighborhood holiday party. Another was spending hours visiting her critically ill daughter in the hospital.

In reviewing her time line, Miriam realized that there were more "hidden helpers"—individuals who contributed to her growth and development—than she had first realized. Among them were her mother, her eldest son, a ninth-grade teacher, her first supervisor, the head nurse at the hospital where her daughter lay dying, a favorite aunt, and a motivational speaker at a conference she had attended.

She realized how much her thinking had changed over time. Instead of letting change happen to her, she learned how to deal with change and ultimately became a change agent for others. She became a "can-do" person, taking responsibility for her own life through accepting risks and daring to dream.

Completing the time line exercise, as shown in Exercise 1.1, made her cognizant of how many individuals had helped her on her journey. "I never realized how privileged I've been; I knew on some level, but not to this extent. I was both overwhelmed with gratitude and feeling a need to reconnect with some of these people. I also was clearer as to why I wanted to be a mentor. I needed to give back some of the gifts from others that I'd been privileged to receive."

Time Line Reflection on Mentoring

In *Composing a Life* (1989), Mary Catherine Bateson describes her developmental journey through life as a composition of connections with women friends. The women, who are part of the composition of her life, flow in and out of her life at different stages, times, and places. Each has contributed to making her who she is. She reminds us that "the past empowers the present, and the groping footsteps leading to the present mark the pathways to the future" (p. 34).

Exercise 1.2, a continuation of the previous one, invites you to reflect on what you have learned from the mentors who have been part of your life's composition and to explore how that learning might affect you as a mentor.

The Mentee's Journey

Madeleine had never given much thought to her mentoring experiences after they were over. She had moved to the Southwest after thirty years as a real estate broker. In a matter of months, she became active in her condominium association and was elected one of its officers. After eight years of chairing the association board, she was eager to move on, but there were no

EXERCISE 1.1

Constructing a Journey Time Line

Instructions: The line in the box below represents your journey as an adult from the past to today. Draw a journey time line like this horizontally on a sheet of paper.

```
┌──────────────────────────────────────────────────────────────┐
│                                                                │
│   ──────────────────────────────────────────────────────      │
│                                                                │
└──────────────────────────────────────────────────────────────┘
```

1. Using words, symbols, or drawings, sketch your journey on the time line. In the space above the time line, note significant life events that influenced you the most, as well as milestones and transitions along the way. Do not feel constrained to stick to work-related events or even those that have to do with mentoring. Focus on events, milestones, and transitions (positive and negative) that have had an impact on your development.

2. Turn your attention next to the space below the time line:

   - Identify opportunities that made a difference in your life and helped you grow and develop.

   - Identify obstacles that got in the way of your journey.

   - Note "unexpected delights"—events and experiences that were not planned but just happened.

3. Review your time line of events, and insert the names of individuals along the way who contributed to your development.

4. What were critical learnings and changes in your thinking?

5. What new learnings emerge for you as you review your time line of experience?

EXERCISE 1.2

Reflecting on Your Time Line

Instructions: Think about your mentoring experiences and the people who were there to guide you, support you, and strengthen you.

My mentors were:

At what point along your journey did they come into your life?

What were those experiences like?

What wisdom have you gained from each of your mentors?

What did you learn about being a mentor?

What is it you learned that might contribute to your own development as a mentor?

What did you learn about being a mentee?

apparent successors with previous experience or knowledge of property management issues. In order to develop a new generation of leadership quickly, she and her board agreed to set up strategically paired mentoring relationships with future association leaders.

When Gordon heard about the vacancy on the board, he immediately volunteered to serve. He stated that he "was looking for something to keep him busy" and thought that this opportunity might be "just what he was looking for." Madeleine was not convinced that he was the one to provide the necessary leadership but was outvoted by her fellow officers. It was her opinion that Gordon was "a nice enough person" but just looking to fill up his time. She was concerned about gaps in his knowledge of issues and problems and offered to mentor Gordon.

Madeleine spent a week putting together an agenda and materials to orient Gordon to what she felt he needed to know. When she presented her list to him, he was affronted.

It turned out that Madeleine's assumptions about what Gordon knew were erroneous. Gordon was the former owner of two construction companies and held an M.B.A.; his son managed properties for a living. Gordon's learning needs were not the same as Madeleine's had been because his experience was different from hers. Had she known more about her mentee's journey before she prepared an agenda and materials, their relationship could have started on a more positive note.

It is human nature to project our own experiences and reality onto someone else. We naturally make assumptions about others and their experiences. Sometimes, with relatively little information, we fill in blanks. Mentors need to guard against this temptation and be aware of what sets the mentor's journey apart from the mentee's journey.

Exercise 1.3 asks you to think about your current or prospective mentee's journey. Use a pencil to complete it because the data you probably have now, particularly if this is a prospective mentee, will be incomplete.

The intent of the exercise is to help you gain a better sense of place about the person you are mentoring, not to construct a detailed complete time line as you did in the previous exercise. If you already know something about this person, it offers an approach for testing out your own assumptions and gaining a clear understanding of factors that may affect the learning relationship.

One way to avoid the tendency to use a one-size-fits-all approach when mentoring several individuals simultaneously is to think about the answers

EXERCISE 1.3

Mentee Time Line

Instructions: What do you imagine your mentee's journey has been? Start with the present and work backward. Think broadly, filling in known milestones, experiences, and events along the time line in the box.

1. What more do you need to know about your mentee in order to have a better sense of his or her journey?

2. If there is more information that you need, what questions will you ask your mentee? What information can you gather from other sources?

3. What insights does your mentee's journey raise for you about your mentee's readiness to learn?

to the questions in Exercise 1.3 and as a result become aware of your knowledge gaps about a particular mentee's developmental journey. Completing this exercise serves to identify potential needs and conversation starting points. If you have difficulty filling in the time line because you have very little information to go on, it may be a cue to gather some baseline data from the individual you are mentoring by asking relevant questions to fill in the gaps. Once you have had a conversation with your mentee, you should be able to complete the mentee journey time line.

Journey of Self and Other

The journey of the mentoring relationship is a journey of self and other and thus is innately complex. It is important to preserve the differentiation and not attempt to homogenize journeys, for "work relationships of any kind are enlivened by difference combined with mutual commitment" (Bateson, 1989, p. 78). The journey time lines in Exercises 1.1 and 1.3 suggest a sense of place about yourself and your mentee. Exercise 1.4 is the third piece of the journey triptych. This time you will consider where you are on your journey time line relative to where your mentee is or will be and the implications of the gap in facilitating learning.

Niles started his career as a schoolteacher and subsequently switched to city government, where he worked for ten years. As a community service volunteer, he was a mentor in a school-to-work program. He attempted to fill out the mentee time line (Exercise 1.3) with the information he had been given prior to his first meeting with Juliana, a prospective mentee. He completed the exercise as fully as he could, and after his first several conversations with her came back to it, filling in the missing pieces. When he completed the exercise to his satisfaction, he felt more prepared to complete the journey worksheet (Exercise 1.4), and as a result, he was able to bring an enlightened perspective to the mentoring relationship.

Niles realized that as much as he wanted to be of assistance, the time he had available might not be adequate given the immediacy of Juliana's need. Having recently decided to return to school himself, he needed to prepare to take the required achievement tests in the next few months. Rather than foreclose the opportunity to mentor where he could have been of assistance, he needed to be up-front with the mentoring coordinator who had approached him and also with Juliana. By being candid about his own needs, they were able to identify workable strategies that would meet his time constraints and still fill her needs.

EXERCISE 1.4

Journey Worksheet: Implications for Facilitating Learning

Instructions: Look at your time line in Exercise 1.1 and then at the mentee's time line in Exercise 1.3. Consider where you are right now on your time line in your life and where your mentee will be or is. Then answer the following questions.

1. What concerns and issues does this comparison raise for you as a mentor? Are there significant differences in your life experiences? Where are the biggest gaps in your experiences?

2. What concerns and issues does the comparison raise for you about your (prospective) mentee's learning needs and learning goals?

3. What specific actions or approaches could potentially have a positive impact on the learning relationship?

4. What specific actions or approaches could potentially affect the learning relationship negatively?

5. What strategies might you use to overcome them?

Once you have completed the journey time lines in Exercises 1.1 through 1.3, you will be prepared to analyze the differences and consider the implications for furthering your mentee's learning.

Using Experience to Ground the Work

Experience and development are intertwined. Using one's lived experience is the text for self-discovery and learning (Lindeman, 1989); it is the most powerful learning resource we have. Mentors who are able to reflect critically on their own experiences and learn from them are best able to model critical reflection in their mentoring interaction.

Barry, an avid golfer, is a case in point of someone who was able to reflect on his own experience and learn from it. Although he now loves the game, he was not always good at it. He had to learn to slow down, concentrate, and maintain focus. In talking with his mentor, he came to the realization that these same principles were his downfall in business and began to make major changes in how he organized and accomplished his projects at work.

Exercise 1.5 provides an opportunity to use the learning you have done in the past to ground your mentoring work. Jot down quick responses in bullet form; then later revisit them more extensively or use the data you generate in conversations with your mentee. If you find that the space provided to answer these questions is insufficient, you could choose to begin a journal with these questions as the topics. You might note words and phrases that first come to mind as you read the questions. You may choose to engage in conversation as a way of addressing the questions. Answer the reflection questions only after you have completed the first four items to your satisfaction. This exercise also asks you to assess the level of difficulty you experienced in addressing these questions. This is a reference point for you as you raise these same kinds of questions with your mentee. For example, if you experience difficulty in answering these questions, you can say authentically to a mentee, "Look, I know these questions are difficult to respond to. I ask myself the same kinds of questions, and frankly it takes me a while to come up with answers that satisfy me. I've found that asking myself about what I've learned from my personal experiences helps me improve my performance."

Angela, a mentor in a distance-learning program who has several student mentees, has found an effective way to help her mentees reflect on their experience. Each time she works with her mentees on a practicum project, she advises them to write in their journals about their learning from the experience. She encourages them to take their learning to the next level by reviewing their entry before going on to the next project. At the end of the

EXERCISE 1.5

Using Experience to Ground Your Work

Instructions: The purpose of this exercise is to provide you with a fresh perspective on how it feels to reflect on experience consciously and to learn from it—what it feels like to "sit at the feet of your own life and be taught by it" (Berends, 1990, p. 8). It will put you in touch with some experiences you have had that can assist you in facilitating the learning of a mentee.

1. Jot down bulleted responses or words that come to mind for questions 1 through 4.

2. At another time, review your answers to see if they trigger additional responses.

3. Complete the reflection questions after you have reviewed your answers.

4. Alternatively, or in addition, you may want to ask mentees to complete this exercise and discuss what the experience of reflecting on experience was like with them. In this way you can position the learning, saying that "part of learning is reflecting on experience; this will give you a preview of what that is like."

---

1. What have you learned from mistakes you have made?

2. What have you learned from your successes?

3. What dilemmas do you face on a daily basis?

4. What are lessons have you learned from those experiences?

Reflection

1. What was it like to address these questions?

2. How would you rate the level of difficulty?

Easy ——————————————————————————————— Difficult

3. What did you learn about yourself in going through this exercise?

second project, she encourages them to make another entry. And again, before beginning the next practicum project, she asks them to review all prior entries.

Seeing Connections

Learning is influenced by past experience and current situations. There is a whole ecology involved in creating a climate for growing. Ecology is the constellation of forces, which is always present, pushing, pulling, and directing our actions in the present moment. Much like an organizational or biological ecosystem, many forces that work on us and make up our personal ecology affect the web of interrelationships within our own personal environment.

The Ecology and Mentoring Connection

We each have a personal ecology—a web of relationships (Helgeson, 1995) and forces at play in our lives at any given moment. For example, Prince is a parent, a son, a biologist, a gardener, a student, a musician, a runner, and a mentor. His work and parenting demands directly affect the amount of time he has available for his mentoring relationship. He is also experiencing internal angst because his mother is ill and his house was recently struck by lightning. Direct and indirect forces like these influence us all the time, whether or not we are aware of them. Exhibit 1.2 illustrates some of the forces around Prince.

Prince's physical dislocation from his home and his angst over an ill parent could very easily affect his role as a mentor. Exhibit 1.3 summarizes all of the impacts on Prince at this time. The impact on his time is considerable, and it may well be that this is the time for him to take a hiatus from the mentoring relationship. On the other hand, mentoring could be a welcome respite from his troubled world right now.

An awareness of a mentee's personal ecology is valuable information. It provides the mentor with helpful clues about when to prod, push, and hold back. It also helps to explain the mentee's reaction, behavior, and thinking.

Identifying Your Own Ecology

Think about the ecology of your own life right now—the web of relationships and forces affecting you. Draw circles or any other symbols or sketches you need to make as full a picture as possible in Exercise 1.6. Then

EXHIBIT 1.2

Prince's Ecology

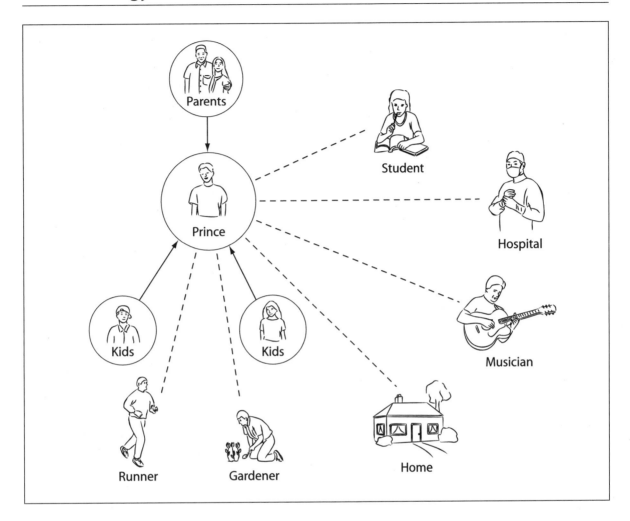

insert arrows (showing a direct impact) and dotted lines (showing an indirect impact) to illustrate the interconnectedness among the symbols or sketches (the forces) you have identified.

If mentors are to facilitate learning of their mentees, they can best begin by being in touch with the forces in their own lives. What else may be going on in your life right now that might affect your mentoring relationship? Consider some of the indirect and direct forces that could affect your mentoring relationship. You may not be able to fill the grid in Exercise 1.7 completely at this time. In that case, come back to it at later.

Increased awareness of the dynamic impact of ecology in a mentoring relationship enables a mentor to look beyond the current mentoring situation.

EXHIBIT 1.3

Impact of Forces on Prince

Force	Direct Impact	Indirect Impact
Mother's illness	Taking inordinate amount of time.	Always waiting for that phone call.
Mentee's needs	Can't give the time I want to the relationship.	Not doing an adequate job or kind of job I'd like to.
Home	Physical dislocation has disrupted my daily schedule.	Can't find anything I am looking for; have to reorder my daily routine.
Parenting	Not being able to spend as much time as I'd like with my children.	Being with my kids makes me feel good. It is a real tonic for me, especially right now!
Gardening	No time. Regret. Miss it.	There is always next year!

Possible Impact in a Mentoring Relationship

Negative. Much as I want to do this, there is no way I can do this without feeling guilty about not doing something else.

Mentors can expand their understanding of the forces affecting mentoring partners by getting to know their mentee and contemplating the various forces that could affect their interaction in the mentoring relationship. This awareness helps in anticipating bumps in the road along the way.

Getting to know a mentee does not mean knowing everything about that person. Rather, gaining a good sense about who this person is and what he or she brings to the learning relationship will help the mentor connect and facilitate a more meaningful learning experience. Listening well and asking thoughtful questions are often enough to elicit the relevant information. Some mentors make notes at the end of each mentoring session about events, special people, or concerns the mentee has talked about and identify specific points of connection for the next mentoring session. Mentors who understand the power of experience and ecology are better prepared to facilitate learning relationships.

EXERCISE 1.6

Your Personal Ecology

Facilitation

In addition to their expertise and experience, mentors need to be familiar with specific process skills in order to facilitate the learning process effectively. Facilitation is a relatively new concept, rooted in principles of adult learning that are largely attributable to the work of Malcolm Knowles (1980). Although frequently labeled as a soft skill, facilitation is a requisite process skill for those who mentor adults. *Facilitation* is difficult to define. *Enable* is the word that probably comes the closest to describing the dynamic interactive process involved in facilitating adult learning.

According to Malcolm Knowles (1980), a facilitator must:

- Establish a climate conducive to learning.
- Involve learners in planning how and what they will learn.

EXERCISE 1.7

Impact of Forces

Force	Direct Impact	Indirect Impact
Possible Impact in a Mentoring Relationship		

- Encourage learners to formulate their own learning objectives.

- Encourage learners to identify and utilize a variety of resources to accomplish their objectives.

- Help learners implement and evaluate their learning.

Mentors facilitate learning in many ways, all the while listening, empowering, coaching, challenging, teaching, collaborating, aiding, assisting, supporting, expediting, easing, simplifying, advancing, and encouraging. "Facilitators of learning see themselves as resources for learning, rather than as didactic instructors who have all the answers" (Brookfield, 1986, p. 63).

There is an inherent flow to the facilitation process. For some learners, this movement takes more time than others. Their lived experience, ecology, and circumstances initially require more support and direction. For others, less support is required because there is more readiness and comfort with the process of facilitation.

The self-reflection on facilitation in Exercise 1.8 provides an opportunity for you to think about the process of facilitation. Think about your experience in facilitating someone else's learning or your observations of someone else in that role.

Acknowledging Learning Styles

According to Brookfield (1986, p. 64), "One important element in facilitating adult learning is helping learners become aware of their own idiosyncratic learning styles." Learning style refers to the pattern of preferred responses a person uses in a learning situation.

The exercises in this chapter, and throughout the rest of the book, provide opportunities to draw on the many unique experiences, problems, situations, and motivations that mentors bring to learning and to use that knowledge to promote effective learning relationships. How the exercises will be experienced will vary according to learning style.

Being knowledgeable about a mentee's learning style has implications for facilitating the learning relationship. That information will assist the mentor in knowing when to step forward and when to hold back, and how to honor specific learning styles that help to facilitate the learning.

Following are some general guidelines that relate to most learning styles:

Pace the learning. The pace of the learning varies and is often interrupted by individual need. Sometimes learners withdraw or avoid when they are uncomfortable. This self-declared time-out is part of the learning process as well and needs to be acknowledged.

EXERCISE 1.8

Self-Reflection: Facilitation

Instructions: Think about your experience in facilitating someone else's learning. Or recall an experience of someone you observed facilitating another person's learning. Then answer the following questions.

1. Describe an experience in which the goal was to facilitate someone else's learning.

2. What did you do? What did the learner do?

3. What were the factors that affected the success or derailment of your efforts?

4. What lessons did you learn from that facilitation experience?

5. What metaphor best describes how that experience felt for you?

6. What, if anything, would you do differently in facilitating your mentee's learning?

Time the developmental intervention. Mentors need to understand where their mentees are developmentally. They cannot assume readiness. That is why partnership preparation is so important. Without establishing an open and candid relationship, it is easy to make erroneous assumptions.

Work toward collaborative learning. Collaboration is creative work. "People labor together in order to construct something that did not exist before the collaboration, something that does not and cannot fully exist in the lives of the individual collaborators"(Peters and Armstrong, 1998, p. 75).

Keep the focus on learning. Mentoring is not a chemistry contest. The partners should not get hung up on personality issues. Stick with the main attraction: learning.

Build the relationship first. The learning will follow. Too often mentors and mentees do not make the time to create the appropriate climate for learning.

Structure the process. Sharing the responsibility for structuring the learning relationship (even in an informal learning relationship) improves the quality of the interaction.

Support, Challenge, and Vision

Effective mentors use a variety of techniques to ensure that the mentee is appropriately challenged and that there is the opportunity to capitalize on different learning strengths. Daloz (1999) identifies three components of an effective mentoring relationship: support, challenge, and vision.

Support is a prerequisite for enabling mentoring relationships. Daloz (1999) describes support as "the activity of holding, providing a *safe space* where the student can contact her need for fundamental trust" (p. 209). Mentors can preempt possible stumbling blocks by identifying when and where they may need to provide support.

Challenge is sometimes referred to as a creative tension that seeks resolution, a stretch opportunity, or a threat. When mentors shortcut the learning cycle by providing answers, they shortchange the process that takes place as mentees seek to discover their own answers by meeting the challenge before them. Feedback is the most powerful tool for assisting learners in meeting challenges. It provides the means for engaging in discussion, setting up dichotomies, constructing hypotheses, and setting high standards (Daloz, 1986).

The importance of vision in mentoring is underestimated. Mentors provide vision in a variety of ways. Role-modeling specific behaviors is one way. They also provide the long view by reminding us of tradition and the road yet to come into view. Because they have been there, mentors often know the coming attractions. They also hold up the mirror of self-awareness, which results in extending the vision of the mentee (Daloz, 1999).

Strategies for Facilitating Learning

There are specific things mentors can do to facilitate mentee learning. The five strategies listed below are particularly useful.

Asking Questions

Asking questions causes an individual to reflect and thereby encourages learning. Asking questions that require thoughtful answers (like those in the exercises in this chapter) is helpful in getting mentees to articulate their own thinking and identifying questions to stimulate thoughtful reflection. The questions can open up a learning conversation or shut it down. Ethical questioning is a must (staying within the bounds of role-appropriate questions). Without it, it is easy to exceed limits of appropriateness and fairness.

What You Can Do

- Ask questions that support and challenge—for example: "That's a nice way of describing the culture. How would you apply some of that thinking to the staff?"

- Ask questions to stimulate reflection—for example: "Could you tell me a little more about what you mean by . . . "

- Allow time for thoughtful reflection—for example: "It sounds as if we've only begun to scratch the surface. Let's think about this some more and discuss it further in our next conversation."

Reformulating Statements

Mentors who rephrase what they have heard clarify their own understanding and encourage the mentee to hear what it is they have articulated. This offers an opportunity for further clarification.

What You Can Do

- Paraphrase what you heard—for example: "I think what I heard you saying was . . . "

- Continue the process of rephrasing and paraphrasing until you are clear and the mentee is no longer adding new information—for example: "My understanding is . . ."

Summarizing

Summarizing reinforces the learning, is a reminder of what has transpired, and allows checking out assumptions in the process.

What You Can Do

- Share the content of what you have heard, learned, or accomplished— for example: "We've spent our time today . . . During that time we . . . As a result, we achieved the following outcomes . . ."
- Leave judgments and opinions out when you summarize.
- Deal with the facts of the situation, not the emotions.

Listening for the Silence

Silence provides an opportunity for learning. Some individuals need time to think quietly. Silence can also indicate confusion, boredom, or even physical discomfort.

What You Can Do

- Don't be afraid of silence.
- Encourage silence.
- Use the silence as an opportunity for reflection—for example: "I notice that whenever we started to talk about . . . you get kind of quiet. I'm wondering what that is about."

Listening Reflectively

So often we hear but do not really listen. When you listen reflectively, you hear the silence, observe nonverbal responses, and hold up a mirror for the mentee.

What You Can Do

- Be authentic—for example: "What I'd like to see is . . ."
- Clarify—for example: "What do you mean by . . . ?"
- Provide feedback—for example: "You did a great job with that. I like the way you . . . I also thought that . . . Next time you might try . . ."

Using Reflection to Facilitate Learning

The role of the mentor is to facilitate learning in such a way that the knowledge, skills, or competencies connect to action in the present and possibility in the future. This requires building on the learner's experience, providing a conducive environment for learning, and appropriately challenging, supporting, and providing vision for the learner.

When the mentor's work is solidly grounded in principles of adult learning, mentor and mentee are viewed as co-learners who both benefit and grow from the relationship. It is a process of becoming for both partners. "In the end it is important to remember that we cannot become what we need to be by remaining what we are" (De Pree, 1989, p. 87). Although we want to encourage mentees "to look, look again," we also need to be diligent observers of the process ourselves. The next chapter broadens our understanding of the dynamics of the learning process by exploring the role of context and its influence in the mentoring relationship.

CHAPTER 2

Working the Ground
Considering Context

Connections are made slowly, sometimes they grow underground.
You cannot tell always by looking at what is happening.
More than half a tree is spread out in the soil under your feet.
—MARGE PIERCY, "The Seven of Pentacles"

Context can be defined as the circumstances, conditions, and contributing forces that affect how we connect, interact with, and learn from one another. It is an elusive and difficult concept to grasp since it is situational and complex. It is situational, because of its lack of generalizability to all contexts, and complex, because we are never in solely a single context.

Think for a moment about the multilayered contexts that accompany you on a daily basis: your workplace, your profession, your social situation, your upbringing, your country or family of origin. What is considered appropriate in any one of these contexts or situations may or may not be appropriate or even welcome in another. We react to the expectations of each context in which we operate based on our own unique (and thus contextual) experience and history. We simultaneously create and bring a context to relationships, and the context of the partnership individually influences on our relationship. Individually and collectively, we respond to contextually derived behaviors and values, and the context or environment also responds to us (Daloz, 1986).

Context is always at play, in subtle and overt ways. It helps us understand the values that drive our behavior, affects our emotions, and colors how we read a person or a situation. Ignoring context, overlooking it, or taking it for granted dramatically affects the learning that takes place in a mentoring relationship. "Adult learning is best understood when the context is considered with the same attention as the teaching and learning interactions occurring within it" (Merriam and Caffarella, 1991 p. 306).

Shawn was a "military brat" and lived in five different countries during his school years. As a child and young adult, he never questioned authority and was very disciplined and self-directed. His initiative, punctuality, and discipline worked to his competitive advantage while he was going through engineering school. Once he started working, however, he found that individual initiative, punctuality, and discipline were less valued. His company had an open-door policy that encouraged co-workers to come and go as they pleased. Building relationships was given high priority, and success was measured by the quality of the team's effort.

We can readily see the layered contexts at work in the disconnects Shawn is experiencing. If he were engaged in a mentoring relationship, it would be helpful to know where Shawn's family context and work reality collide. This understanding would enable his mentor to facilitate a mentoring experience in which the learning is more relevant and the learning process engaging. For example, they might describe a number of approaches to solving a problem and explain why using one is more effective than another.

Mentoring relationships exist across as well as between contexts. For example, many educational institutions have well-entrenched mentoring programs for fledgling teachers, and many graduate schools offer graduate education using mentoring as a vehicle to support, promote, and accelerate learning (across contexts—in this case the context of education). Community mentoring partnerships foster economic development between business and education (between contexts). Senior centers offer opportunities for cross-generational mentoring (between contexts). The array of mentoring opportunity is as varied as the contexts themselves.

The context of a mentoring relationship adds its own unique layer of complexity. Is the relationship formal, informal, sponsored, incidental? Is it part of a program? Does the relationship operate in a group context? Is it a one-to-one partnership? Because multiple contextual layers affect an individual simultaneously, learning partners in a mentoring relationship need to communicate expectations and establish ground rules and processes that work for them in specific context. Otherwise they may find themselves operating at cross purposes.

All mentoring is embedded in context. Effective mentors consciously develop context sensitivity, which aids in understanding perceptions of the mentoring operating within it. (For an in-depth treatment of context and its relationship to learning, see Merriam and Caffarella, 1991.)

The scope of possibilities for discussing the subject of context in relation to mentoring is very broad indeed. Long distance, cross-cultural, cross-gender, and cross-generational mentoring are the most familiar. Of these, cross-gender and cross-generational mentoring have probably received the most attention in the literature. In this chapter, however, the focus is on two other mentoring contexts: long distance and cross-cultural relationships. The reason is the explosion of interest and increased participation in both global and long-distance types of mentoring relationships, often simultaneously and synergistically. The reality is that in today's increasingly global world, learning cannot always be tied to a full-time-access relationship (Bell, 1996). The urgency for addressing these two topics is even more pronounced in the specific contexts of long-distance and cross-cultural mentoring. (The fact that cross-gender and cross-cultural mentoring are not being discussed in this chapter does not make them any less significant. In fact, they add additional contextual layering to both long-distance and cross-cultural mentoring relationships.)

Long-Distance Mentoring

Long-distance mentoring is a geographically diverse mentoring relationship that takes place when it is not feasible, desirable, or convenient for mentoring partners to meet on a regular face-to-face basis. It is not unusual for a relationship to start out as a face-to-face partnership and to become a long-distance mentoring relationship at some point along the way.

Who has not been engaged in a relationship when there has been a geographic distance between the primary people in it? Do you have a college roommate or high school classmate with whom you still keep in contact? Perhaps your siblings or other family members live a distance away. Maybe you do business regularly with someone in another country. Or you could be involved in an intimate relationship at a distance.

Long-distance contexts present multiple issues and challenges. It may be that you and your former high school classmate live in different hemispheres, and finding the right time to talk across time zones is a challenge. You and your friend may not be able to connect on a regular basis.

Reflecting on any long-distance relationships can provide valuable insights. The process of discovering personal challenges to long-distance relationships provides a window for reflection on your own experience, which in turn helps in applying that knowledge to long distance mentoring relationships.

Exercise 2.1 is provided to help you in that process. To complete the exercise, focus on any existing or previous long-distance relationship. Identify the challenges you have faced in the relationship. Use the left-hand column in the exercise to develop a list of the challenges you have faced. When you "meet" with your mentee, ask about challenges that she had to overcome in creating and sustaining relationships, and jot these down in the right column. With completed grid in hand, discuss with your potential mentee the implications of these long-distance experiences (both successes and failures) for your mentoring relationship. What will work? What will not?

You may have had to learn how to articulate a problem to someone outside your immediate environment or situation, or to overcome resistance to technology to maintain the relationship. It may be challenging for you because you do not have a sense of what else is going on at the other end of the line while you are engaged in conversation. Because you cannot see each other, you may find that it is hard to know what the other person is feeling or thinking. These same kinds of challenges extend to long-distance mentoring relationships.

Long-distance relationships present special challenges to mentoring partners. As mentors and mentee travel from place to place across time zones, creating other venues for connection becomes important. It could be that a large challenge is overcoming a five-hour time differential and finding a mutually agreeable time to schedule a conversation that works well for both mentoring partners.

In the case of someone you know, it is likely that you are already comfortable in the relationship about asking him or her about what is happening. Even separated by time and space, you still continue to engage in a mutually satisfying relationship because you have an established connection. This is not the case in long-distance mentoring situations, where mentoring partners may not have even met one another.

Creating the Relationship

Eric had been engaged in an on-line discussion with Tom. They connected regularly on the Web and had several stimulating exchanges. Eric had also been in touch with René, who had recently published a thought-provoking article. Eric contacted René and began an e-mail exchange. Before long, Eric realized he was engaged in two parallel conversations that might be

EXERCISE 2.1

Issues and Challenges in Long-Distance Relationships

Instructions:

1. Complete the left half of the grid by listing the challenges you have faced in creating and sustaining long-distance relationships in general.

2. Gather the same information from your mentee to complete the right half of the grid.

3. Discuss the implications of dealing with long-distance issues and challenges for your mentoring relationship. Determine ways to overcome the negative issues and challenges and maximize the positive issues and challenges in a long-distance mentoring relationship.

Mentor	Mentee
Generic Issues and Challenges	**Generic Issues and Challenges**

enriched by broadening the dialogue to include both Tom and René. When he broached the idea to Tom and René, they were enthusiastic and they began to "meet" on-line. The synergy among them was apparent, and they mutually decided to establish a peer mentoring relationship. But when the pace of contact escalated, Eric could not keep up with it. Soon the flurry of chat time slowed down, and after several more weeks there was barely a whisper. Neither Tom nor René took the initiative, in Eric's absence, to maintain it. Several months later, Eric realized he missed the connection and tried to resuscitate the relationship but found it was too late. He could not breathe any life back into it.

Regular contact is necessary but not sufficient. There should be mutual consensus about the meaning of "regular" and a decision to adhere to that agreement. Tom, René, and Eric missed an opportunity to ground their learning relationship. Had they discussed what would work for each of them instead of falling into a pattern, they might have found a workable solution. They were unable to sustain the pace they had created. Had there not been "too much too soon," they might have stood a better chance of continuing to benefit, participate, and nurture the relationship.

Weaving Real Connections

Without establishing a connection with others, mutual understanding cannot be achieved. Distance relationships endure because there is connection; a relationship has been forged, and common ground has been established. From that basis, common understandings flow, which then become the basis of the relationship. An understanding of each other's context contributes to the success of that relationship. The goal is to seek balance in whatever venues are chosen.

The challenge is to find an electronic format that will work and to be open to using multiple technologies as they emerge. The growth of the World Wide Web, for example, has led to a variety of electronic long-distance options referred to variously as on-line mentoring, cybermentoring, e-mentoring (electronic mentoring), and telementoring. Currently these terms are being used interchangeably. (There is considerable variation in how these options are being implemented.) Some are called mentoring but are more like listservs or on-line discussion. The key to successful long-distance mentoring is taking time to establish the human connection and develop a relationship. Generally listservs and on-line discussion do not include that opportunity.

Many mentors underestimate the time commitment required to establish and build long-distance mentoring relationships. In general, time is a major factor in establishing, building, and sustaining mentoring relationships. In long-distance mentoring, making the connection is a formidable task and requires time and tending.

Marsha, a midlevel administrator at a remote office location of a large midwestern university, has held several administrative positions over the past five years. She has never been involved in a formal mentoring relationship but now realizes that she needs one to gain visibility and knowledge about university politics, and to develop contacts and skills because she wants to move quickly into a higher-level administrative position. She is a firm believer that building relationships is the key to success.

Robert, a full professor and dean of the health science school located on the main campus has agreed to be her mentor. Marsha and Robert have had several telephone conversations since their mentoring relationship began, but each one has been increasingly frustrating for Robert. Inevitably Marsha is late for the calls and despite generous apologies has not managed to call once at the appointed time. By the time she reaches him, Robert has switched his attention to other matters and needs time to shift gears so that he can focus on the conversation.

The conversations are always the same: Marsha apologizes for her tardiness and steers the conversation toward questions she has about university news, people, and the weather. Robert answers her probing questions but feels wrung out from her questioning and experiences little satisfaction from the conversation.

The example illustrates several of the time and connection dilemmas common to long-distance mentoring relationships. Although Marsha is getting her information needs met, Robert is feeling more like a data source than a mentor.

A long-distance mentoring relationship requires planning to use the time well. Robert needs to make sure that ground rules for communication are established. He and Marsha should have discussed these and agreed on them at the beginning of the relationship. And although Robert was trying to attend to his conversation with Marsha, he may not have been really hearing because he was frustrated by her behavior and was still processing what he was working on when Marsha's telephone call interrupted him.

Robert failed to check out his assumptions about why Marsha was late. He assumed that punctuality was not important to her. Perhaps being late is the norm in her department. Robert needs to be more candid in revealing his own thinking and feeling. If he were clear about the goals of this mentoring partnership, he would be able to facilitate learning by refocusing Marsha on her goals. What appears to have happened here is that Marsha's goals were overridden by her information needs. By focusing the conversation on preparing and negotiating the relationship, each would develop more realistic expectations about it.

Without a discussion of context, it is impossible to be sensitive to the immediate needs of the partners engaged in a relationship. By making time at the end of a conversation for summarizing and debriefing the conversation, frustration could be lowered. This is an opportunity to discuss satisfaction with the learning and talk about ways to achieve better results.

Points of Connection

Long-distance mentoring depends on meaningful points of connection. Points of connection are the building blocks for effective interaction. By connecting first, we are better able to develop fruitful and productive learning relationships. Exhibit 2.1 names and explores these venues.

Robert never set the climate for learning (Point 1). He took on the responsibility of mentoring Marsha in good faith. He thought Marsha had great potential and wanted to help her. By talking about her learning needs and his own time demands, Robert could have probably avoided some of his frustration (Point 2). He knew little about Marsha. Certainly he knew her "on paper" and had met her at a recent retreat, but he really did not know who she was as a person. There were many communication options available to Marsha and Robert, in addition to the telephone (Point 3). Perhaps some of the "information" questions (where appropriate) could have been taken care of by e-mail. Delays in making a scheduled contact are also points of connection for conversation (Point 4). Had expectations been set more clearly, Marsha would have realized that she needed to call Robert to let him know she was running late. Robert then would have the option to renegotiate the time frame. Some of Robert's frustration could have been alleviated had he checked on the effectiveness of the communication from the very beginning (Point 5). Perhaps learning is going on for Marsha, but Robert has no sense of what that is and, for his part, feels that it is the "wrong kind" of learning. They have not had the learning conversation (Point 6). Information is being shared at the expense of interaction (Point 7).

Communication Success Strategies

Long-distance mentoring communication often gets accomplished in sound bites—a quick e-mail, a fax, or a quick conversation. At other points, longer

EXHIBIT 2.1

Points of Connection

What to Do	How to Do It
Invest time and effort in setting the climate for learning.	Determine mentee learning style and learning needs.
Be sensitive to the day-to-day needs of your mentee.	Spend time connecting with your mentee. Ask enough questions to give you sufficient insight into your mentee's work context.
Identify and use multiple venues for communication.	Explore all available options: e-mail, videoconference, new Web-based technologies, telephone, mail, and emerging technology—and use more than one. Look for opportunities to connect face-to-face, even at a long distance.
Set a regular contact schedule, but be flexible.	Agree on a mutually convenient contact schedule, and make sure it works for you and your mentee. If you need to renegotiate a scheduled appointment, use that situation as an opportunity for connection and interaction.
Check on the effectiveness of communication.	Ask questions: Are we connecting? Is the means we are using working for us? Is it convenient?
Make sure that connection results in meaningful learning.	Is learning going on? Is the mentee making progress?
Share information and resources—but never as a substitute for personal interaction.	Set the stage to share information. Then share the information and follow up once the information is shared.

conversations or exchanges take place. Knowing which to use and when to use it is advantageous.

Mentors can monitor the communication that takes place by following these guidelines:

- Actively listen.
- Check out assumptions about what is going on periodically.

- Share thoughts and feelings candidly.
- Maintain sensitivity about the mentee's personal and learning needs.
- Discuss accountability and follow up regularly.
- Reflect on the learning taking place.
- Focus on the mentee learning goals.

Exercise 2.2 provides a reflection tool for mentoring communication. It can be used after each mentoring session or periodically throughout a mentoring relationship. (A mentoring session can be face-to-face interaction, a telephone call, or on-line communication.) The tool is most helpful when mentoring partners complete this form and use it as a basis for discussion.

Cross-Cultural Mentoring

The culturally constructed nature of relationships surfaces in cross-cultural mentoring relationships. The juxtaposition of one's values with those of someone else affects the interaction taking place in a learning relationship. How the word *mentor* is culturally understood could alter the very essence of the relationship. For example, the word *mentor* might be closely related to *teacher, supervisor,* or *expert* in another cultural context. It might not translate directly, or it could connote negative association because of a perception that it is a position of weakness to seek a mentor.

Cross-cultural barriers consist of more than just language or semantic barriers. There are sometimes barriers of distance, which affect the relationship as well. But the biggest chasm is cultural and has to do with how one sees the world as well as how one acts within it. For example, in China, the role of teacher is traditionally revered in the Confucian order of hierarchy and status ranking. In this instance, one's perception of the teacher might affect openness and directness of communication or how conflict is resolved. The idea of accountability is also linked to cultural perceptions. In some cultures, the expectation is that the teacher must initiate contact, and communication is tied to credibility and control. If the words *teacher* and *mentor* are interchangeable terms in that culture, the implications are obvious.

Mario Lombard, the distribution manager for an Italian winery, was eager to move from Italy to his company's corporate offices in the United States. To prepare himself, he found a U.S. manager who was an experienced and knowledgeable insider who agreed to be his mentor. His mentor, Nancy, was looking to expand her leadership skills and saw mentoring Mario as an opportunity to broaden her own cultural awareness.

EXERCISE 2.2

Long-Distance Mentoring Interaction Reflection

Instructions: As you reflect on each of the questions below, focus on your most recent mentoring session. This reflection is most effective when the mentee completes a copy of it as well and the mentoring partners then discuss their reflections and develop action strategies together.

1. What went particularly well during our mentoring session?

2. What relationship challenges did we face?

   • Were we communicating effectively with each other?

   • Were we candid and open in our communication?

   • Did we take care to check out assumptions with each other?

   • Were we actively listening to each other?

3. What learning challenges emerged?

   • What did we do to hold ourselves accountable for the learning?

4. What logistical challenges affected our communication?

   • Were the venues (e-mail, telephone, meetings) we have selected working for us?

   • Were there external factors, such as time and access, that affected our interaction in any way?

5. What three strategies could improve the quality of our mentoring interaction?

   •

   •

   •

6. What is the action plan for implementing each of the three strategies?

The relationship did not go the way Nancy had hoped. Right from the beginning, each encounter with Mario was fraught with tension. Mario would ask good questions but constantly interrupted her as she attempted to provide answers. His frequent emotional outbursts became a constant irritant. When Nancy found herself beginning to doubt his intention, she decided to do some research about his culture.

Culture has a lot to do with how people express themselves. Nancy learned that Mario's emotional responses were a result of a culture where subjective feelings are valued. Mario's need for discussion was not about her but actually the way he was able to gain clarity. She realized that her own need for results did not match Mario's need for process.

Peter Jensen, an executive in a fast-expanding publishing business, and his mentee, Liu Pei Wen, talked on the telephone initially and agreed to conduct mentoring sessions through videoconference (Liu Pei Wen was located in Beijing, and Peter's office was in the United States). Peter set up a meeting and confirmed the time for the videoconference with Liu Pei Wen. In the meantime, her manager had asked her to attend a meeting with him, which was scheduled at the same time as the prearranged videoconference with Peter. When Peter called in for the videoconference and found that Liu Pei Wen was not there, he decided that something must have happened and that he would wait to hear from her. After two days passed and Peter had not heard from her, he called Liu Pei Wen to ask if something was wrong. She apologized profusely for the misunderstanding. When Peter offered to set up a meeting for the following morning, Liu Pei Wen responded that she needed to "recommend it to her manager."

The example of Liu Pei Wen and Peter Jensen demonstrates the reality of many cultures where the understanding of time means different things in different cultures. For Liu Pei Wen, punctuality was not as important as honoring hierarchy.

In mentoring relationships, it is important to spend some time in the early part of the relationship talking about how the relationship will proceed. In cross-cultural relationships, especially those that are cross-cultural and long distance, time should be set aside to talk about areas in which there may be cross-cultural misunderstandings, for example, in regard to values and time.

In general, effectiveness in a cross-cultural mentoring relationship rests on four elements: a mentor's cross-cultural competency, a flexible cultural lens, well-honed communication skills, and an authentic desire to understand how culture affects the individuals engaged in this relationship.

Cross-Cultural Competency

Global and cross-cultural experts identify an array of competencies for establishing successful global relationships in business (American Society for Training and Development, 1999). Many of these pertain to mentoring relationships as well.

Become Culturally Self-Aware

Self-knowledge is the most important intercultural competency for a mentor to possess. Like a compass, self-knowledge keeps the mentor on course and focused. Those who become conscious of their own values and assumptions and critically examine them (Mezirow, 1978) will be rewarded with a deeper understanding of their own behavior. We become aware of personal cultural biases by getting stuck in someone else's cultural assumptions.

Strategy. Identify culturally derived values and assumptions that could affect your relationship. It may be that you were brought up in a culture where sharing feelings is inappropriate or that a one-on-one learning relationship is seen as weakness. What values and assumptions do you hold that someone might not readily understand from a culture other than your own?

Develop a Working Knowledge of and Appreciation for Other Cultures

It is easy to get locked into our own ways of thinking. We begin to believe and act as if these are the best or even only ways of thinking and behaving and shut down with regard to other ways of doing things. Getting locked in someone else's stereotypes in mentoring is just as possible and troublesome as it is in any other context. Mentors who are in the best position to facilitate learning are willing to learn about the basic functional elements of their mentee's culture.

Strategy. Seek information about your mentee's country and its people, politics and government, key historical and cultural achievements, dominant religious beliefs and practices, family and social structure, educational system, economics and industry, geography, sports, entertainment, and symbols.

Improve Communication Skills

Listening and speaking are critical aspects of any mentoring relationship and all the more so in a cross-cultural mentoring relationship. Initial enthusiasm and excitement in learning are often followed by a period of confusion and frustration. In a cross-cultural relationship, this confusion may be exacerbated by poor communication skills. Being a good communicator requires a high level of interpersonal skill and respect for cultural practices.

Strategy. Ask open-ended questions. Be comfortable in the silences. Paraphrase and reflect feelings and content. Repeat and rephrase. Check for understanding by asking what specific words, phrases, or expressions mean. Avoid examples that are regionally or culturally specific. Whenever possible, use universal examples and be as descriptive as possible. A universal example is generic in the sense that it can be understood across cultures. Topics might include the weather, education, career, hobbies, travel, and family. Keep in mind that phrases that are commonplace in one country may be difficult for others to understand (for example, "put up with," "butt of a joke").

Become Culturally Attuned to Other Cultures

This means being able to "read the culture" of a mentee and understanding what is happening and what is expected through the context and nonverbal behaviors. Through conversation, mentor and mentee become aware of different perceptions and values that could facilitate or hinder their communication. These values inform the expectations and agreements that will flow out of the relationship. One partner's cultural expectations may be results oriented. This may not be true for the other partner. Decision making in some cultures takes several meetings to achieve. Waiting for consensus may be difficult for one partner personally and yet may be very much a part of the way another culture conducts its business. Joking between men and women in some cultures is considered inappropriate.

Strategy. Be aware that people from other cultures do not always express their feelings verbally. Avoid asking questions that are personal, embarrassing, or probing. *Kiss, Bow and Shake Hands* (Morrison, Conaway, and Borden, 1994) describes the customs, business practices, cognitive styles, protocols, greetings, and behaviors for sixty different countries and is an excellent reference for those engaged in cross-cultural mentoring.

A global mind-set gives mentors the ability to expand their own knowledge and deal more effectively with the complexity of the global world. They will begin to appreciate the need to be flexible and know that they must continually strive to be culturally sensitive.

Developing a Flexible Cultural Lens

A mentoring relationship in a cross-cultural context requires preparation. One cross-cultural expert, Gloria Sandvik (personal communication, 1998) identifies four action strategies for maintaining a flexible cultural lens: prepare, remember, observe, and show. For each, she offers specific recommendations. An adaptation of her work in Exercise 2.3 provides a concrete to-do list.

Mentors must be prepared but must also recognize that there is a great deal of individual variation within a particular cultural context and very diverse people within any culture. Each individual is still a composite of learning styles, family values, economic circumstances, and so forth. "The key to cross cultural mentoring is knowing that you must also add all of the complexity of any human interaction after somehow becoming culturally attuned" (M. Oyler, personal communication, November 1999).

Communication

Communication is the essential building block for facilitating learning relationships and ensuring a successful cross-cultural mentoring experience. The checklist in Exercise 2.4 is designed to help you assess your comfort in relation to many of the communication skills needed in cross-cultural mentoring relationships. In order to make the best use of the checklist for your own learning, follow these steps:

1. Assess your comfort on each skill.
2. Review any items you assess at a level of moderately comfortable (M) or uncomfortable (U).
3. Determine what skills you need to work on.
4. Prioritize the skills you have identified according to what you need to work on the most.
5. Separate your priorities into short-term and long-term concerns.
6. Develop a plan.
7. Seek feedback on the plan.
8. Revise the plan accordingly.
9. Set target dates for completing the plan.
10. Get started.

It is easy to get lulled into complacency in a relationship, especially when things appear to be going well. To keep yourself cross-culturally fit, reflect on the items in Exercise 2.5 whenever you engage in a cross-cultural mentoring experience.

EXERCISE 2.3

Intercultural Communication Checklist

Use this checklist to guide communication in a cross-cultural mentoring relationship.

1. Prepare

    ____ Research your mentee's culture before you meet.

    ____ Check your intention. What do you want from this relationship?

    ____ Clarify the goals of the mentoring relationship.

2. Remember

    ____ Use active listening skills (that is, clarifying and confirming).

    ____ Show interest, attention, and empathy.

    ____ Respect differences in learning pace, and respect silence.

    ____ Experiment with different approaches, questions, and expressions.

    ____ Suspend judgment.

    ____ Before concluding on any point, clarify meaning and support connection using descriptor questions (who, what, when, how, how much, how many).

    ____ Express your need to think about something and get back to the person so that appropriate reflection and research might be pursued.

    ____ Be patient.

    ____ Accept differences.

3. Observe

    ____ Your own assumptions, biases, and stereotypes.

    ____ Consistency and relevance in responses and feedback to make sure that adequate communication is taking place.

    ____ Your own values and the underlying contrasting values that might be operating in the relationship.

    ____ Any discomfort, disconnects, or feelings that might be at play.

4. Show

    ____ Respect.

    ____ Reliability.

    ____ Expertise and knowledge.

    ____ A learner-centered focus.

Source: Sandvik, 1996. Adapted with permission.

EXERCISE 2.4

Cross-Cultural Mentoring Skills Inventory

Instructions: For each skill in column 1, indicate how comfortable you are in using that skill by checking one of the three grids in column 2: very comfortable (V), moderately comfortable (M), or uncomfortable (U). In column 3, identify an example that illustrates a concrete situation when you were either comfortable or uncomfortable using the skill. Insert a check mark in column 4 for each skill that you feel you need to improve to develop a comfort level. Once you have completed the skill inventory, rank your overall comfort level on a scale of 1 to 5, with 5 being the most comfortable and 1 being the most uncomfortable.

Column 1	Column 2			Column 3	Column 4
Skill	V	M	U	Examples	Needs Work
Reflective listening (using the skills of attending, clarifying, and confirming)					
Checking for understanding					
Maintaining cultural self-awareness					
Providing and receiving feedback					
Maintaining global perspective					
Reading between the lines (keying into feelings)					
Suspending judgment					
Maintaining emotional versatility					
Exercising cultural flexibility					
Creating culturally appropriate networking opportunities					
Modifying communication style to accommodate cultural differences					
Sensitivity to varying cultural perceptions to time, space, authority, and protocol					
Overall Comfort Level	1	2	3	4	5	

EXERCISE 2.5

Questions for Self-Reflection on Cross-Cultural Mentoring Relationships

Instructions: Make several copies of this worksheet. Answer each of the questions as candidly and fully as you can. Periodically complete this form again, and compare your answers over time. Notice any changes. If you are engaged in a cross-cultural mentoring relationship, you should notice positive change each time you complete this self-reflection. If you are unable to complete these questions to your satisfaction, perhaps you should reevaluate your involvement in a cross-cultural mentoring relationship.

1. Number of hours I have devoted this month specifically aimed at learning another culture:

2. How I am furthering my learning (for example, by taking a trip, attending a workshop, coaching):

3. What I learned:

4. Mistakes I am making and learning from:

5. What I am doing to modify my communication style to accommodate cultural differences:

6. What I am doing to read nonverbal messages (such as pauses and silences):

7. What I do when I find myself in a culturally inappropriate situation:

8. How I am doing at really suspending judgment in my mentoring relationship:

   What helps me is:

   What gets in the way is:

Authentic Desire

Having an authentic desire to learn about another culture requires an openness and willingness to listen without making value judgments about what is being heard. Mentors must genuinely want to understand how culture affects the unique individuals engaged in the mentoring relationship. If mentors are not making mistakes and talking about these cultural mistakes in their relationship, they are not learning. Remember to give yourself and your mentoring partner permission to make mistakes and then create ways to learn from mistakes together.

Reflecting on Context

Context is a formidable consideration in facilitating the learning that takes place in mentoring relationships. For mentors, consideration of context is a requisite part of the preparation tool kit. Context is an intimate part of who we are. We bring contextual layering to our relationships—and, in fact, to everything we do. Consciously reflecting on context helps ensure integrity of the learning process. The chapters that follow explore the broad concepts of communication, time, and ground rules introduced in this chapter in more depth.

CHAPTER 3

To Everything
There Is a Season

Predictable Phases

Under a sky the color of pea soup
she is looking at her work growing away there
actively, thickly like grapevines or pole beans
as things grow in the real world, slowly enough.
> —MARGE PIERCY, "The Seven of Pentacles"

entoring relationships progress through four predictable phases: preparing, negotiating, enabling, and coming to closure. These phases build on one another to form a developmental sequence, which varies in length from one relationship to another.

The concept of phases in mentoring relationships is not a new one (Kram, 1988; Phillips-Jones, 1982; Missirian, 1982). The phases I present in this chapter, and more fully describe in Chapters Four through Seven, however, are less bound by time definition and psychological milestones and more focused on the behaviors required to move through each of the stages Regular reflection throughout the duration of the mentoring relationship empowers the mentor's learning, which in turn informs, and potentially strengthens, the facilitation process. Reflection, in combination with the key elements of readiness, opportunity, and support, forms the scaffolding (or structure) for facilitating the learning that takes place throughout each phase.

The Phases

Preparing, negotiating, enabling, and coming to closure are part of every mentoring relationship, formal and informal. Awareness of the phases is a key factor in successful mentoring relationships. When they are taken for granted or skipped over, they can have a negative impact on the relationship. Simply being aware of them provides significant signposts.

Movement through the four phases follows a fluid yet predictable cycle, and usually has some overlap between phases (see Exhibit 3.1). Thus, during the enabling phase, when mentoring partners are most likely to face potential obstacles (perhaps a geographical move), they may need to renegotiate aspects of their mentoring partnership agreement in order to move forward and maintain the relationship.

Preparing

Each mentoring relationship is unique. So each time a new mentoring relationship begins, both mentor and mentee must prepare individually and in partnership.

Tilling the soil before planting can involve a number of processes (Piercy, 1982): fertilizing, aerating, cultivating, plowing, and so on. Similarly in the preparing phase of a mentoring relationship, a variety of processes take place. Mentors explore personal motivation and their readiness to be a mentor. They assess their mentoring skills to identify areas for their own learning and development. Clarity about both expectation and role is essential for establishing a productive mentoring relationship.

Preparing is also a discovery process. The mentor evaluates the viability of the prospective mentor-mentee relationship. A prospecting conversation with the mentee assists in making that determination. This initial conversation then sets the tone for the relationship.

Negotiating

Successfully completing the negotiating phase is like planting the seeds that lead to the fruition of the mentoring relationship. Planting seeds in well-cultivated soil produces growth. Negotiating is the business phase of the relationship—the time when mentoring partners come to agreement on learning goals and define the content and process of the relationship.

EXHIBIT 3.1

The Phase Cycle

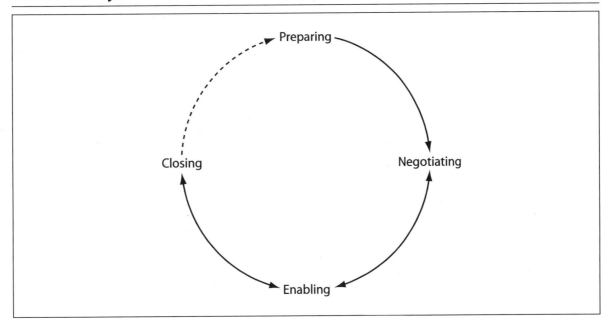

Negotiating is not as simple as drawing up an agreement. A key part is the conversation that leads up to it, when the ground rules for moving the relationship forward are developed. The negotiating phase has more to do with creating a shared understanding about assumptions, expectations, goals, and needs than actually putting a formal agreement in writing. It involves talking about some of the soft issues in a relationship—topics like confidentiality, boundaries, and limits, which often are left out of mentoring conversations because the partners find these issues difficult to talk about. Although some individuals are concerned that such a discussion undermines trust, it actually lays a solid foundation for building trust.

Another way of describing the negotiating phase is "the detail phase." This is when the details of when and how to meet, responsibilities, criteria for success, accountability, and bringing the relationship to closure are mutually articulated.

Enabling

The enabling phase takes longer to complete than the other three phases since this phase is the implementation phase of the learning relationship, when most of the contact between mentoring partners takes place. It is complex. Although it offers the greatest opportunity for nurturing learning and development, the mentoring partners are also most vulnerable to myriad obstacles that can contribute to a derailment of the relationship.

Even when goals are clearly articulated, the process well defined, and the milestones identified, every relationship must find its own path. The enabling phase is a process of path building: maintaining a sufficient level of trust to develop the quality of the mentoring relationship and promote learning. Effective communication is key.

The mentor's role during this phase is to nurture the mentee's growth by establishing and maintaining an open and affirming learning climate and providing thoughtful, timely, candid, and constructive feedback. Both the mentor and mentee monitor the learning progress and the learning process to ensure that the mentee's learning goals are being met.

Coming to Closure

Coming to closure is an evolutionary process that has a beginning (establishing closure protocols when setting up a mentoring agreement), a middle (anticipating and addressing obstacles along the way), and an end (ensuring that there has been positive learning, no matter what the circumstances). All three components are necessary for satisfactory closure.

A relationship may start out splendidly, with the mentoring partners respecting each other, sharing mutual interests, and developing good rapport. Suddenly the spark goes out. When this happens, mentors often find that working their way back through the phases (see Exhibit 3.1) enables them to evaluate and refashion a stalled relationship into a productive and mutually satisfying experience. Being aware of signals that indicate it is time for closure helps to ensure a timely and positive closure.

Closure involves evaluating, acknowledging, and celebrating achievement of learning outcomes. Mentors, as well as mentees, can benefit from closure. When closure is seen as an opportunity to evaluate personal learning and apply that learning to other relationships and situations, mentors leverage their own learning and growth and reap the full harvest of the relationship.

Using the Four-Phase Model

In *Tuesdays with Morrie* (1997), Mitch Albom describes an extraordinary relationship with his former mentor and coach, Morrie Schwartz. Albom and Morrie had reestablished contact after many years and because of their previous history determined that they had a mutuality of interest in continuing the relationship (*preparing*). Morrie, who was Albom's teacher, was dying from Lou Gehrig's disease, and his time and energy were at a premium. Albom and Morrie decide to meet regularly, every Tuesday (*negotiating*). For fourteen Tuesdays after their reunion, Morrie shared the wisdom he had gathered over the years (*enabling*). Throughout the relationship, they prepared for *closure*, knowing that closure would happen when Morrie died. Although they were unaware of it, their relationship followed the predictable four phases.

If you use the four-phase model, you will find that being aware of the signposts of each phase tends to keep you on a steady course. Each phase poses its uniquely specific questions. Complete the checklists at the end of each of the next four chapters will help you ascertain your readiness to move on to the next phase. In addition, reflecting on learning offers an opportunity to assess and monitor progress, record learnings, and keep the focus on learning goals as you and your partner move through the various phases of your relationship.

Reflecting on Learning

Learning is not only the end result of a mentoring relationship. It is an integral part of the ongoing mentoring experience, starting during the preparing phase and continuing until closure is reached. It is introduced here because of its power to inform the facilitation that takes place during every stage.

Research indicates that one of the ways adults learn best and also retain the knowledge they learn is by consciously reflecting on their learning. Reflection is an introspective dialogue carried on in written form that stimulates the raising of questions, provokes the assessment of learning, and enables the integration of new learning. In addition, reflection during the mentoring process "enables us to slow down, rest, and observe our journey and the process of self-knowledge that is so important along the way" (Huang and Lynch, 1995, p. 57). As a result of reflection, the mentor is in a better position to assist the mentee in "the integration of learning and the framing of mechanisms for deriving meaning" from experience (Alpine, 1992, p. 15).

Regular mentoring reflection has the following benefits:

- Clarifies thinking
- Captures the richness of learning experiences

- Helps to sort out the mentor's feelings about what is occurring
- Provides a written log with specific details and information
- Promotes systematic and intentional reflection

Exhibit 3.2 identifies strategies for successful reflection.

Some mentors find that including factual material (such as notes capturing the content of the conversation) as well as reactions, feelings, and process notes (notes about what one was thinking at a particular point in time) helps them reflect on their mentoring experience. Others record their mentee's progress in achieving articulated learning goals. Through this process, they find that reflection informs their mentoring conversations by revealing questions and issues to pursue with their mentees.

Each mentor should choose an approach to reflection that works for him or her. For those who prefer a qualitative impressionistic method, writing a regular diary entry is helpful. Others prefer the ship's log method, which charts specific details of the relationship. Sentence-completion stems can stimulate the flow of thoughts and ideas. Progoff (1975), for example, uses a three-step process:

EXHIBIT 3.2

Strategies for Successful Reflection

1. Include the following material:
   Factual material
   Reactions
   Feelings
   Process notes
   Goals

2. Write regularly.

3. Use the approach that works best for you:
   Dear Diary ...
   Ship's log
   At first ... And then ... And now ...
   What stands out for me is ...
   Questions on my mind ...

4. Get started.

1. Begin reflection with the phrase "at first." Write a paragraph or two.

2. Switch to "and then," writing whatever comes to mind.

3. Follow with completion of the sentence stem: "and now."

The following example shows how one mentor used this approach following his initial mentoring session:

> At first, *when I met Dani, I was put off. She seemed flighty, and even the way she dressed seemed to say, "Don't take me seriously."* And then *we started talking, and I was amazed at the depth of her insights and breadth of her experience. She knew far more than I had given her credit for.* And now *I am looking forward to working with her and learning from the diversity of experience she brings to the relationship.*

Regular reflection requires discipline throughout the phases. It is easy to procrastinate when it comes to recording reflections unless you make it a habit. The best advice is just to get started. With practice, it gets easier.

The reflection triggers in Exhibit 3.3 are particularly useful immediately following a mentoring session.

EXHIBIT 3.3

Sentence Stem Reflection Triggers

1. About my mentee:

    What I am thinking:

    What I am wondering:

2. My most difficult mentoring challenge so far:

3. What is working well:

4. What could be working better:

5. A new learning that has affected me:

Some Tips on Reflection

- Schedule regular reflection. Engaging in reflection regularly is more important than the time spent on this activity.

- Personalize the format (for example, use bulleted items).

- Try not to get bogged down in detail. Capture a brief description or note some specifics. Make sure you have written enough, so that when you review your entry at another time, you will be able to recall the mentoring experience clearly.

- Note your feelings at the time. Remember that whatever it is that you experience or that stimulates your thinking will help you better understand your own behavior.

- As you write, note frustrations, learnings, curiosities (ruminating questions), and magic moments (peak experiences or synchronicities).

- Especially write about particularly meaningful mentoring that you have observed or experienced.

- If you find yourself grasping for straws, sit down and write anything, even if it is that you have no thoughts. Reflect on why that is so. You may find that all you needed was a starting point. Once you have begun, it is easier to continue the process.

Reflection is a tool that can be used to stay the course and focus attention on the relationship and learning. The next section presents a diagnostic and reflective tool that works in tandem with reflection to enable the mentoring relationship.

Readiness, Opportunity, and Support

Every phase of the mentoring relationship presents specific learning challenges. The combination of three primary elements—readiness, opportunity, and support (the ROS model)—facilitates successful movement through each phase. *Readiness* relates to receptivity and openness to the learning experience. It addresses the issue of preparedness for every phase. *Opportunity* refers not only to the venues, settings, and situations available for fostering learning but also the quality of that opportunity. *Support* pertains to relevant and adequate assistance to promote effective learning and builds on the concept of support presented in Chapter One.

When a third party determines the mentoring pairing, readiness is sometimes the last element of the ROS model to fall into place for the mentoring partners. There may be ample opportunity to foster learning, and the mentor may be able to provide adequate support, but the mentor or the mentee, or sometimes both, may not be open to this particular relationship at this time. Many reasons can account for lack of readiness—for example, lack of perceived need, a belief that the need for mentoring is regarded as a weakness, or that the teachable moment has not yet arrived or has already passed. Charging headlong into a mentoring partnership when readiness has not yet been achieved spells disaster. Situations like this can be overcome by allowing adequate time for both parties to come to a shared understanding of the purposes of the relationship before moving into the negotiating phase.

The three elements of readiness, opportunity, and support together form the framework for the ROS tool to help mentors and their mentees diagnose what elements are in place and analyze what elements are missing before moving onto the next phase of the mentoring relationship. Gauging the presence or absence of these primary elements helps keep the mentoring relationship on track by identifying possible stumbling blocks. For example, before moving into the enabling phase, mentor and mentee must make sure that they have completed the necessary groundwork, have some ground rules in place, are clear about the purpose of the relationship, have determined the opportunities for enabling the relationship, and understand the kind of support that is required.

Use the ROS tool in Exercise 3.1 as a checkpoint before moving to the next mentoring stage or when the relationship seems somewhat out of kilter. This grid is helpful in identifying strengths and weaknesses in the relationship and assists in targeting areas for improvement of the relationship.

Exhibit 3.4 illustrates how one mentor used the ROS tool to determine that he and his mentoring partner were not yet ready to move into the negotiating phase of the relationship. Although he knew this was the situation, completion of the grid helped him pinpoint some areas for discussion with his mentoring partner during their next conversation.

An Investment of Time

Facilitating effective learning relationships requires not only an awareness of the four mentoring phases, reflection on the mentoring experience, and taking the key elements into account but also an investment of time. Mentors who are familiar with the predictable phases, understand the scaffolding necessary to support learning, and take into account the multi-

EXERCISE 3.1

The ROS Tool

PREPARING	Mentor	Mentee	Mentoring Partners
Readiness: Receptivity to learning			
Opportunity: Settings and venues to foster cognitive, affective, and relational learning			
Support: Appropriate, relevant, and adequate assistance to facilitate effective learning			
NEGOTIATING			
Readiness: Receptivity to learning			
Opportunity: Settings and venues to foster cognitive, affective, and relational learning			
Support: Appropriate, relevant, and adequate assistance to facilitate effective learning			
ENABLING			
Readiness: Receptivity to learning			
Opportunity: Settings and venues to foster cognitive, affective, and relational learning			
Support: Appropriate, relevant, and adequate assistance to facilitate effective learning			
COMING TO CLOSURE			
Readiness: Receptivity to learning			
Opportunity: Settings and venues to foster cognitive, affective, and relational learning			
Support: Appropriate, relevant, and adequate assistance to facilitate effective learning			

EXHIBIT 3.4

Using the ROS Tool to Reflect on the Preparation Phase

	Mentor	Mentee	Mentoring Partners
Readiness: Receptivity to learning	Have had prior experience mentoring and am looking forward to the experience once again.	Not sure. Don't know mentee very well. Not yet clear about expectations.	Not enough time spent together yet to determine if we are ready to move into the negotiation phase. Don't have a good handle on this yet.
Opportunity: Settings and venues to foster cognitive, affective, and relational learning	Limited personally, but I have lots of good contacts and networks I can tap into.	Worried about opportunities to apply learning on the job.	I have a few ideas about this. May be able to bring mentee along to board meetings as an observer. Want to introduce her to a variety of people.
Support: Appropriate, relevant, and adequate assistance to facilitate effective learning	I feel pretty good about this.	I need to check out how much support my mentee feels he is going to need.	We are going to need to talk about boundaries around this.

dimensional dynamics of time that have an impact on the relationship dramatically enrich the quality of the mentoring experience.

Lack of time is the most frequently articulated reason attributed to failure in a mentoring relationship. Here is what a teacher mentor had to say about how time affected her relationship:

> It wasn't her fault. It was mine. I thought I was committed. It was only when I tried to schedule time and couldn't find any of it that I realized mentoring wasn't enough of a priority for me at this time in my life.

Time is a pervasive issue throughout the mentoring relationship. It needs to be considered in the preparation process (particularly self-preparation), discussed in the negotiation process, honored and monitored during the enabling phase, and adhered to in the coming to closure phase. Because of its impact throughout a mentoring relationship, time merits special attention.

Making the Commitment

Landis (1990) reminds us that "the key to success may ultimately be the selection of mentors who are dedicated to mentoring and are willing to spend the time necessary." In fact, time entails more than willingness and dedication, or even meeting time. It needs to be a commitment.

All mentors must make sure that their enthusiasm, willingness, and desire are not clouded by rose-colored glasses before they commit to mentoring. They must take the time to discuss the prospective mentee's background and other relevant information to see if there is a fit and understand that mentoring is an investment of time, with the actual time depending on the mentee's goals and needs. Before committing to a mentoring relationship, a mentor should be prepared to block off a realistic amount of time and protect that time.

After Sharon, a very popular mentor and one of few women of color in a senior leadership position in her company, evaluated her time commitments, she realized that she could not devote more time to mentoring than she had already allotted. Now she takes anyone who asks her to be a mentor out for a one-time lunch. During that time, she asks questions to ascertain the person's career and mentoring goals and provides recommendations about other mentors.

Keeping Time in Perspective

Time is a pervasive concern in each phase. Compounding the time issues idiosyncratic to mentoring are time issues related to work, personal demands, and life in general. Distance mentoring relationships take more time and energy, particularly in the early phases of the relationship. Dealing with time concerns up front and in ongoing fashion helps mentors and mentees maintain perspective so that they can focus better on the learning goals.

Mentors who do not hold a conversation about time commitments with their mentees may find that their relationship gets sabotaged early on. The words of this busy manager-mentor demonstrate the value of holding a frank discussion of how to deal with time-related problems: "We spent time discussing background and information and planning to make sure that we would be able to make this relationship work for us. We both have tight schedules and wanted to make sure that we utilized the windows of time we had."

Using the negotiating phase to address time expectations and time constraints that might be problematic for the relationship can help to prevent later misunderstandings.

Developing a Time-Sensitive Attitude

Once the negotiation phase is over, the enabling work begins. It takes time to develop, nurture, and sustain a trusting and open mentoring relationship. The attitude about the time spent mentoring is critical.

Ultimately mentors will spend less time overall on the relationship if they effectively manage the time they do have by following these guidelines:

- Avoid the pitfalls of mentoring on the run, such as sandwiching mentoring in between meetings, multitasking, and giving advice without taking time to explain the context (Bell, 1996).

- Encourage your mentee to use the available time constructively and maximize time spent together by coming to the meeting prepared.

- Start each session with a progress review or update to help you regain focus.

When Time Becomes an Issue

It takes time to sustain a learning relationship. Time becomes an issue when the partners cannot find enough of it, acknowledge a need to call time out, or do not use the time they do have wisely:

Finding time. You may think you do not have enough time, or you could be procrastinating because you begrudge the time spent on the mentoring relationship. In this situation, step back and ask yourself why it is you cannot get started or continuously postpone. Perhaps you are assuming too much—or too little. You may view your mentoring obligation as bigger than it is.

Calling time out. Call time out if you need it to give the relationship space. Reflection and contemplation are necessary for real learning. The importance of the pause as a transforming moment (Loder, 1989) should not be overlooked. You may find that you need to build in time to let new learnings sink in, gel, and come together or to let new ideas emerge.

Using time consciously. Often we are unaware of how we spend our time. Finding the time is one thing; using it well is another. Consciously reflecting on the time spent mentoring provides insights for process and content learning.

Irene's goal is to become an entrepreneur, and she is interested in learning how to get started. Martin has a reputation as the entrepreneur's entrepreneur, and Irene was delighted he agreed to mentor her. But after three months of meeting together, something in their relationship seemed to be amiss. Martin completed the mentoring time pie in Exercise 3.2 and discovered two things that surprised him: he and Irene have not spent enough time on exploring topics that would help her meet her goals, and he has not

EXERCISE 3.2

Mentoring Time Pie

Instructions: The circle below represents the totality of the time you and your mentee spend together. Divide the circle up into blocks of time to illustrate how you spend your time. In completing this circle, consider the topics you discuss and the various venues for learning. Then answer the questions that follow.

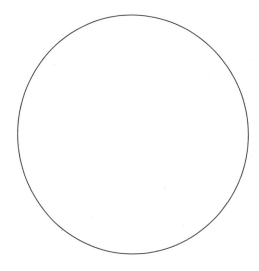

1. What can you learn from this circle about the quantity and quality of time you spend in your mentoring relationship?

2. What would you like to do less of?

3. What would you like to do more of?

4. Look at the circle again from the perspective of the percentage of time you spend talking and the amount of time your mentee is speaking. What do you learn from that analysis?

5. Identify three ways you can improve the quality of the time you spend on this mentoring relationship.

really let Irene participate actively in the relationship. He realizes that he has been grandstanding and she has been the passive listener.

At their next meeting, Martin shares his circle with Irene and asks her what she thinks. Together they talk about how they might strengthen their relationship. As a result, Martin learns something about himself and is also able to facilitate Irene's learning more effectively.

The circle in Exercise 3.2 represents the totality of your mentoring relationship time. Divide it into sections based on how you spend your time in the mentoring relationship. Check out your perceptions with your mentee's perceptions.

Developing a strategy helps mentors use their time wisely. The dynamics of time involved in a mentoring relationship are not always straightforward. The following strategies promote successful time management in a mentoring relationship:

Schedule time in advance. Always try to get a date on the calendar. If you need to postpone a mentoring session, do it, but make sure you schedule your next one when you do. Used wisely, a calendar reminder is a point of contact for communication.

Monitor your time. Be aware of the amount of time you are spending on mentoring (also in proportion to your other tasks). Acknowledge when you are pressed for time, but do not put mentoring on the back burner.

Spend quality time. Recognize the importance of time in the mentoring relationship. Especially be aware of how you spend your time in the relationship because that is far more important than the quantity of time you spend together. When you are present, be fully present. Plan to use the time well.

Take care of yourself. Make time to work on your own growth and development. We often think about what we can do for others through mentoring, but this is an opportunity to optimize personal development too. In addition to the time you will need to spend with your mentee, consider the time you will need to receive training, hone skills, and get feedback from your mentee.

A Recap

Facilitating effective learning relationships requires a mentor's commitment to time and investment of time during the entire mentoring cycle. Reflecting on one's own learning and tending to the key elements of readiness, opportunity, and support to make sure that they are in place helps mentors promote the learning of their mentees. Familiarity with the predictable phases in the cycle is a critical part of the mentor's tool kit.

CHAPTER 4

Tilling the Soil

Preparing

A thicket and bramble wilderness to the outside but to us
Interconnected with rabbit runs and burrows and lairs.
—MARGE PIERCY, "The Seven of Pentacles"

T hings often look quite different on the outside than from an inside perspective. Perhaps that is why preparing is the most overlooked phase in the mentoring relationship (Zachary, 1994a). From the outside, a mentor might assume that subject expertise and experience are adequate preparation for becoming a mentor. Someone who has been a mentor before might assume that preparation is unnecessary, even a waste of time. The reality on the inside, however, is quite different. The preparing phase is critical to building and maintaining the relationship and forging the connections that sustain the relationship over time. Taking time to prepare for a mentoring relationship provides a significant learning opportunity for the mentor and the mentoring partnership.

Assuming Too Much

Mentors who assume the mentor role without adequately preparing themselves or their relationship are often disappointed and dissatisfied. The example of Cynthia and Fran illustrates what can happen when two people serendipitously fall into an informal mentoring relationship and fail to prepare themselves for the relationship.

Fran, a superstar, leader, and political maverick, is articulate, bright, and energetic. Cynthia, a former journalist a decade younger, is every bit as bright and energetic. When introduced at work, they liked each other instinctively and immediately connected around similar interests and hobbies of volunteer work, writing, and hiking.

As they got to know each other better, Cynthia came to respect and admire everything about Fran: her drive for success, her individuality, and her leadership style. When Fran invited Cynthia to join her project team, Cynthia was both surprised and flattered because she had already mentally adopted Fran as her role model of the successful woman leader. Cynthia commented at the time, "Here was an opportunity looking me right in the face—a chance to learn new skills and at the same time to be mentored by someone whom I respect and hope to emulate."

Fran viewed Cynthia as her younger counterpart, her earlier self revisited. She admired Cynthia's ideas and innovations, and especially Cynthia's eagerness to please and her palpable hunger for success. She decided to help accelerate Cynthia's development.

Cynthia was delighted that Fran wanted to mentor her and worked hard to please her. She gave time and energy freely, without limits. The result of the collaboration between Cynthia and Fran was exciting to them both. Their talents complemented each other, and the products they developed together were impressive. Cynthia was continuously learning new skills. Fran was pleased because she benefited professionally and personally from Cynthia's efforts.

In time, Cynthia developed her own reputation for innovation and high-quality performance. As she did, Fran became increasingly possessive of Cynthia's time and effort. As Fran's demands escalated, Cynthia became frustrated, and a list of unaddressed topics grew, eroding the trust between them. The relationship became clouded with emotion and mixed signals. Still, Cynthia remained loyal to Fran and continued to meet and even exceed her increasing demands, but she began to resent Fran. She felt that she owed Fran her loyalty and did not want to hurt her, but, she said, "I felt as if she was extracting everything from me. I was giving her my best, and she was swallowing it and me up. At times I felt as if I was a piece of property that she owned. At other times I felt conflicted."

You might argue that Fran and Cynthia were never really mentoring partners, even though Fran called herself Cynthia's mentor. There was no active individual or partnership preparation. Although they were filling mutual needs, the needs were never explicitly discussed (and probably never even implicitly examined). They took the relationship for granted, never acknowledging the mentoring nature of their relationship. Their assumptions about the relationship remained untested. They used each other to satisfy their individual professional needs and never discussed their relationship or the changes that had taken place.

Thoughtful preparation of a mentoring relationship can avoid the pitfalls Cynthia and Fran experienced. Preparing for a mentoring relationship is akin to tilling the soil before planting: it creates fertile ground before seeds are planted in order for the roots to take hold and support the tree or plant.

This chapter focuses on self-development in preparation for the mentoring role and provides a framework and tools for engaging and connecting with the mentee. The tools can be used as actual tools or as a point of departure for self-reflection or partnership conversation.

Mentor Preparation

For the most part, mentors do not deliberately think about preparing themselves in advance for the mentor role. Formal mentoring programs usually provide some assistance and training prior to assuming the role (which is usually not very effective in furthering self-preparation because of the limited time available). Those who are mentoring on their own, however, are not likely to consider self-preparation before meeting with a prospective mentee.

Motivation drives participation in a mentoring relationship and has a direct impact on behavior, attitude, and emotional resilience in mentoring relationships. Reflecting on motivation before engaging in the relationship can affect the quality of the interaction within it. Mentors who have a deep understanding of why they are doing something end up more committed to it. Because of that focus of their energy, they do it better, and probably save time in the long run.

Understanding motivation requires introspection and candor. We all have internal and external motivations for doing things. We are sometimes unaware of the former until we need to articulate them. And in regard to the latter, even though we verbalize them, they are not always as perceived. We may think that one reason is motivating us, but when we look beyond the presenting reason we come up with new understanding.

There are many reasons for becoming a mentor: the satisfaction of passing on knowledge, helping to build a business, expanding someone else's knowledge base, achieving recognition, receiving reward for the effort, increasing one's own productivity, expanding one's personal network, getting known, repaying the debt of what others have given to one, and being in a position to exert positive influence.

Lester, a rising star in a training and development department of a public utility company, had just asked Sylvia, a twenty-three-year veteran in the department, to be his mentor. He admired how easily she was able to develop training curricula and how facile she was on her feet. He hoped to have the same abilities himself someday.

Sylvia was ambivalent about accepting the invitation to mentor him. Although she felt a sense of duty, she knew that was not sufficient reason to say yes. As she began exploring her motivation, she realized much of it was externally driven, based on what others expected of her. She did like the feeling of having others seek her out for advice (which her coworkers frequently did). She did find helping others personally rewarding; for example, she could point to multiple coworkers whom she had influenced at some point in their careers. But now she was feeling the limits of her own knowledge. In looking for opportunities to further others' learning, she had been neglecting her own, and she was not confident that she could adequately fill Lester's learning needs.

Before Sylvia considered Lester's invitation, she decided that she needed to learn more about his learning goals to determine if his goals would fit with her experience and knowledge.

Understanding Mentor Motivation

Exercises 4.1, 4.2, and 4.3 build on each another and offer an in-depth approach for understanding self-motivation. You may be tempted to write them off because they appear to be the same, but once you start working on them, you will find that they come at motivation from different angles.

Exercise 4.1 represents several broad commonly articulated motivations. You might think that it would be hard to imagine anyone answering no to these questions, because most people, at least to some extent, would like to believe that they have the qualities addressed in the exercise. But note that because the exercise asks for specific examples, it forces concrete and candid evaluation.

Motivation may be tied to conditions of a particular relationship or external pressures. On one level, it may feel like an organizational imperative or a voluntary engagement (or both). The underlying question is, What is driving your participation? As with most questions in life, the presenting reason is not always the underlying reason. Discovering core motivation is a little like peeling back the layers on an onion and finding even more lay-

EXERCISE 4.1

Mentor Motivation Checklist

Instructions: For each item below, put a check in the "yes" column if the reason listed reflects why mentoring appeals to you. If it does not, put a check in the "no" column. Following each item, list concrete examples to illustrate your answer.

Reasons That Mentoring Appeals to Me	Yes	No	Examples
I like the feeling of having others seek me out for advice or guidance.			
I find that helping others learn is personally rewarding.			
I have specific knowledge that I want to pass on to others.			
I enjoy collaborative learning.			
I find working with others who are different from me to be energizing.			
I look for opportunities to further my own growth.			

ers underneath. What you find will depend on how truly candid and self-reflective you can be.

Sally is looking for assistance in developing her fledgling packaging business. Leonard, a retired small business owner himself, has volunteered to mentor her as part of the Small Business Association's business mentoring program. His primary motivation for mentoring her is his felt obligation to give back some of the wisdom he gleaned from other businesspeople who helped him get started. In peeling back his onion, he discovers that his motivation came from a feeling of loneliness and a lack of stimulation; since his retirement, he was no longer interacting with other business owners.

Exercise 4.2 offers an opportunity to pull back the layers and explore motivation further. Complete the first sentence stem stating your primary motivation for being a mentor. This sentence becomes the starting point for the remainder of the exercise. Before you identify your first reason, ask yourself why that was your primary motivation. What is underlying those reasons? This reason now becomes the starting point for identifying the second reason. And your response to the third reason will reflect what underlies the second one. The final step is to analyze your answers to all three reasons and record your observation under the last sentence stem. Exhibit 4.1 demonstrates how Lou, an account manager in a consulting firm, completed Exercise 4.2.

In completing Exercise 4.1 about broad, general reasons and then Exercise 4.2 about more specific reasons below the surface of your stated reason, you may have found that your actual motivation was different or more complex than you originally thought. Or you have found yourself more committed to your original reason by the time you completed the exercise. Now you are ready to look at a potential mentoring relationship and determine if you are ready for this relationship.

Exercise 4.3 affords the opportunity to analyze why you want to participate in the relationship and what it is you can meaningfully contribute to it. It begins where Exercise 4.2 left off, with stating the primary motiva-

Exhibit 4.1

Lou's Motivation for Mentoring

My motivation for mentoring is . . .

I've worked here for 15 years and feel that I have gained important insights that may help accelerate someone else's career development.

Reason 1

Other people have made it possible for me to be where I am today. As a senior leader this is something I need to do.

Reason 2

It is my responsibility to help our employees become better contributors.

Reason 3

I have a particular area of expertise that is in great demand at this time.

My primary motivation for mentoring is . . .

To share what it is I really know and am valued for within the company. I realize that I have a responsibility here. If I don't share my expertise, the company won't have that expertise in its next generation of managers.

EXERCISE 4.2

Identifying Mentor Motivation

Instructions: Complete each of the following sentences. Although you may be tempted to stop after you have identified the first reason, continue to work your way down the page. Consider motivations that might underlie each reason you have identified. When you run out of steam, push yourself a little further or wait until another time and come back and complete this exercise.

My motivation for mentoring is . . .

Reason 1

Reason 2

Reason 3

My primary motivation for mentoring is . . .

EXERCISE 4.3

Assessing Readiness for This Mentoring Relationship

Instructions: Answer each of the following questions so that you are clear as to why you want to engage in this particular relationship at this time.

1. I want to be a mentor because ...

2. I want to participate in *this* mentoring relationship because ...

3. My experience and expertise will contribute to this relationship by ...

4. Specific things I can and am willing to do to help this individual are ...

5. Therefore, I will ...

tion for being a mentor. If in completing this exercise you find that you want to participate in the relationship but cannot add value to it, you may choose to forgo this possibility. Or you may find that you are highly motivated to be a mentor, but this relationship is not for you.

Motivation has an impact on sustainability and commitment. A potential mentor who is not internally motivated is not ready for the relationship or likely to work at sustaining the relationship, facilitating the learning relationship effectively, and ultimately growing from it personally.

Motivation is only part of the picture, however. Mentors need to be comfortable using a wide range of skills.

Mentoring Skill Comfort

It is not unusual to be knowledgeable about specific skills and still not feel comfortable using them. A person who has received training in managing conflict, for instance, is not necessarily proficient at or comfortable in using those skills. Moreover, the extent to which this person feels comfortable affects whether he or she uses the skill.

Mentors who facilitate effective learning relationships are comfortable using an assortment of related process skills. The process tool kit for mentors facilitating effective learning relationships consists of twelve generic skills.

Brokering Relationships

Brokering relationships means skillfully making the right contacts and laying the groundwork for mentees to connect with other people who can be resources to them and provide resources they can use and experiences to further their achievement of learning objectives. In order to broker connections, mentors need to be skilled networkers and have a stable of diverse contacts from whom to draw expertise, resources, and information.

Building and Maintaining Relationships

Too frequently we put great energy into starting a relationship and assume that because of these initial efforts, it will continue to develop on its momentum. In fact, the processes of building and maintaining relationships require tending, patience over time, and persistence. Some people are better at building than maintaining. Mentors need to be adept at both.

Coaching

Coaching and mentoring frequently get confused. As each construct has evolved over time, they have gotten increasingly harder to differentiate.

Coaching is always a part of mentoring, but coaching does not always involve mentoring. Coaching within the context of a mentoring relationship has to do with the skill of helping an individual fill a particular knowledge gap by learning how to do things more effectively.

Communicating

Effective communication is critical to successful mentoring, just as it is in any other relationship. A person can make the best speech in the world, but if no one is listening, what good is it? So it is with mentoring. Facilitating a learning relationship is based on effective communication. Communication is not just centered on sharing knowledge; it depends on many other factors as well, including building enough trust to encourage open communication, being authentic, listening effectively, checking for understanding, and articulating clearly and unambiguously. It also means being able to pick up on what is behind the words being said by another person (the nonverbal cues).

Encouraging

Encouraging in a mentoring relationship takes many forms. It can encompass cheerleading, confidence building, gently pushing at the right time and in an appropriate manner, motivating, and inspiring.

Facilitating

Facilitating is the means by which mentors enable learning. The key elements are establishing a hospitable climate for learning and promoting self-directed learning. The learner is involved in planning, designing, implementing, and evaluating the learning.

Goal Setting

Completion of learning goals is the raison d'être of the mentoring process. Skill in being able to assist a mentee in crystallizing, clarifying, and setting realistic goals is essential.

Guiding

Mentors are guides. They clear a path and prepare the mentee for what it is they are about to see and learn. By role modeling, mentors provide an opportunity for mentees to reflect on what they see. Guides also help maintain focus and help the sojourner reach their destination in safety.

Managing Conflict

Inevitably conflict occurs within any relationship. Managing conflict involves managing a conversation about differing points of view. It does not mean eliminating them. Rather, it is about inviting dialogue to understand varying points of view.

Problem Solving

Problem solving means engaging the learner in the solution of the problem. Mentors do not solve problems for mentees. They provide assistance in the problem-solving process. The goal is to guide that process rather than provide the answer. Mentors must have comfort with problem-solving strategies.

Providing and Receiving Feedback

Feedback is an enabling mechanism throughout the mentoring relationship. Mentors need to know how to provide constructive feedback and assist their mentees in asking for feedback (see Chapter Six).

Reflecting

Reflection is a significant tool for facilitating the growth and development of mentee and mentor. It is the springboard to action and further learning. Being comfortable with the process skill of reflection means being able to step back, evaluate, process, assess, and articulate learning and consider the implication of that learning for future action. Being skillful at reflecting on learning enables a mentor to model that skill for a mentee.

Inventorying Mentoring Skills

The twelve mentoring skills are listed on the inventory in Exercise 4.4. The purpose of the exercise is to gauge your comfort in using each skill and to identify skills you need to develop comfort in using.

Mentoring preparation presents an opportunity for mentors to extend their own learning as well as facilitate mentee learning. As a result of using the mentoring skills inventory, you will have identified areas for furthering your own development and learning. As you progress through the relationship, you may want to seek feedback on how you are doing relative to these skills from your mentee.

Simone did not discover anything she had not already known about herself before completing the mentoring skills inventory. The inventory confirmed her felt lack of comfort managing conflict and reflecting. Her tendency was always to smooth things over and avoid conflict. Taking time to get more comfortable with reflection seemed like a luxury rather than a necessity.

Completing the inventory did raise those skill discomforts to a conscious level and make Simone aware of the areas where she could strengthen her performance as a mentor. She was also somewhat surprised

EXERCISE 4.4

Mentoring Skills Inventory

Instructions: Review each skill in column 1. In column 2, indicate how comfortable you are in using each skill by checking one of the three grids as follows: V (very comfortable), M (moderately comfortable), or U (uncomfortable). In column 3, identify an example that illustrates a concrete situation when you were either comfortable or uncomfortable using the skill. Insert a checkmark in column 4 for each skill that you feel you need to improve to develop a comfort level with it. Once you have completed the skills inventory, rank your overall comfort level with all twelve skills on a scale of 1 to 5, with 5 being very comfortable, 3 being moderately comfortable, and 1 being uncomfortable.

Column 1	Column 2			Column 3	Column 4
Skill	V	M	U	Examples	Needs Work
1. Brokering relationships					
2. Building and maintaining relationships					
3. Coaching					
4. Communicating					
5. Encouraging					
6. Facilitating					
7. Goal setting					
8. Guiding					
9. Managing conflict					
10. Problem solving					
11. Providing and receiving feedback					
12. Reflecting					

Overall Comfort Level	1	2	3	4	5	

when she looked at the skill list and saw that she was moderately comfortable in most areas but not very comfortable in any. Simone jokingly remarked, "I think I need a mentor to mentor me about mentoring."

Prioritizing Learning Needs

Once the mentoring skills inventory is complete, the next step is to prioritize learning needs. In addition to realizing that she needed some mentoring herself, Simone targeted two mentoring skills she wanted to work on: managing conflict and reflecting. Of the two, managing conflict was the more immediate need because it would help her challenge and support a mentee's learning.

The process of identifying one's comfort with various mentoring skills alone may raise one's consciousness enough to help improve effectiveness in a particular area. However, developing and implementing a personal learning plan provides a discipline to help stay the course. The benefits to this approach enrich immediate and future mentoring relationships and potentially transcend the mentoring experience itself.

Exercise 4.5 follows on the heels of Exercise 4.4 as the intermediate step of moving from assessment to action. It provides a place to record those skills that you want to work on and identify some measures for gauging success of your learning.

Crafting a Mentor Development Plan

Simone's first objective was to develop familiarity with the topic of conflict management. She defined reasonable learning objectives for herself and then identified human and material resources and methods to assess her progress. Her strategy was to talk with her coworkers and gather recommendations on what how-to books to read. (In the process of gathering recommendations, she would also have the opportunity to talk with her peers about their preferred methods of managing conflict and get some ideas on ways she could hone her skills.) Once she made her reading selection, her plan was to read several books and apply the strategies as she learned them, gathering feedback from others along the way. Part of the plan was to create a learning log to record her successes and learnings about managing conflict. She decided that this would have the added incentive of helping her develop more comfort with the reflection process, her second objective.

Having defined her objectives, identified resources, and built in ways to assess her progress, Simone drafted a plan, including a realistic timetable for

EXERCISE 4.5

Establishing Learning Priorities and Measures for Success

Instructions: First identify the two or three skills from Exercise 4.4 that you need to work on that would most improve your effectiveness in a mentoring relationship. Then determine how you will measure your success in developing the skills you have identified.

PRIORITIZING THE LIST
1.
2.
3.
Measures of Success for Skill 1
Measures of Success for Skill 2
Measures of Success for Skill 3

accomplishing her objectives. She then sought out colleagues and asked for feedback on her plan. Once she revised it, she started implementing her plan.

Developing Stretch Goals

Stretching is good exercise for the body as well as the mind. It enables us to reach further physically and mentally. The saying, "Stretch yourself today so you'll be in better shape tomorrow" (Pritchett and Pound, 1995, p. 30), rings true as an approach to preparing for the future.

Stretch goals encompass the vision of where you want to be—that is, the challenge before you. Mentors with well-defined stretch goals tend to have a heightened sense of their own learning needs and offer themselves as exemplary role models of self-directed learning.

Stretch goals result from reaching to broaden one's experience base. The difference between where one wants to be and where one is helps define the learning needed to make that journey.

Michael, a new associate in a large law firm, wanted to open a private practice someday. He knew that in order to do that, he needed to learn the business of practicing law. Every year he identified three stretch goals to prepare him to actualize his dream. In year one, he worked on developing his accounting skills. In year two, his goal was to develop professional networks through attending bar association meetings and section meetings in his area of practice. In year three, his goal was to develop skills in legal specialties outside his regular area of practice. Identifying stretch goals is now part of his life. He encourages the partners and associates in his own firm to make that a regular part of how they conduct business.

Exercise 4.6 provides a format for developing an action plan to achieve specific stretch goals, based on the measures of success identified in Exercise 4.5. The mentor development plan may identify as many as three or four stretch goals. For each goal you identify, you will need an action plan. The key to success in filling out the action plan is to define reasonable stretch goals that take you beyond the present moment. Think of stretch goals as a springboard for action. For each goal, define clear-cut objectives, outline activities that will help you bridge the gap, identify the resources you need (and where you can find them), lay out a time frame for accomplishment of the objective, and identify the first step you will take toward achieving that stretch goal. (You may find that you need more room to complete the items than is provided. Add whatever categories you need to enable you to implement the plan.) Building in touch points to evaluate progress provides momentum during the implementation process.

EXERCISE 4.6

Stretch Goal Action Plan

Instructions: Complete an action plan for each stretch goal you have identified. State your goal clearly and identify how you will determine whether you have achieved that goal (measures of success). Then complete the chart.

Stretch Goal:

Measures of Success:

Objectives	Activities	Resources Needed	Time Frame	Next Step

Periodically reviewing the measures of success you identify will keep you on track.

Role Definition

Awareness of motivation, comfort with fundamental mentoring process skills, and commitment to continuous learning all contribute to mentor readiness. When coupled with clear role definition and preparation of the relationship, they create a solid foundation for a rich mentoring experience.

Clarity about role definition is the basis for creating a productive mentoring partnership. Role refers to anticipated or expected functions a mentor might play—for example, team builder, coach, confidant, teacher, guide, or advocate. At different times in a mentoring relationship, different roles are required, often blurring rather than clarifying the mentor's role.

Partnerships that fail frequently fall victim to one of the following difficulties:

Role collusion, which results from taking the role for granted. The mentoring partners unknowingly collude because they do not discuss role expectations and let the relationship coast. "We'll get to it later," they say, and never do. This becomes a vicious circle, and false expectations are set up.

Role diffusion, which results when the mentor has the expectation of being all things to all people. That is, the mentor assumes more roles than may be required or reasonable to expect and assumes the role of caretaker. "Oh, I'll take care of that for you" is the typical response.

Role confusion, which occurs when lines of authority are blurred and there is lack of clarity about disparate and sometimes overlapping roles and conflicting responsibilities. The mentor is also the mentee's supervisor, evaluator, or relative.

Role protrusion, which occurs when mentors inject themselves into situations in which they do not belong, as when a mentor intercedes on behalf of the mentee when it is inappropriate or unwarranted.

All of these role perversions can be avoided if the mentoring partners set aside adequate time to engage in an open, frank, and direct conversation about roles during the preparing phase.

Getting Started on the Right Foot

Andy and Myron fell into a mentoring relationship as they worked together on several nonprofit board committees. Both assumed that holding a specific discussion about their roles was unnecessary. Myron was relying on his mentor, Andy, for hints about how to delegate responsibility and to help him understand more about the political workings of nonprofit organizational life. Andy saw his role as preparing Myron, new to nonprofit work, to take on increasing responsibilities. Their amicable and friendly relationship shifted very quickly when Andy started pushing Myron to sit on the other task forces that he chaired.

Had Andy explored his own mentoring motivation through Exercises 4.1 and 4.2 and assessed his readiness for the role of mentor, he would have been better prepared and gotten his relationship started on the right foot.

Preparing for a mentoring relationship is not time intensive, but it does require dedicated time for reflection. By completing the exercises presented thus far in the chapter, you can help get your relationship off on the right foot. You will need to do the following:

- Reflect on your motivation for becoming a mentor.

- Get comfortable with the mentoring skills you may need to draw on.

- Identify your learning needs, and create a mentor development plan.

- Be clear about what it is you are looking for in a mentoring relationship.

- Consider what it is you are willing to contribute to the relationship.

- Be willing to share your needs, expectations, and limits candidly.

- Prepare for your role as mentor, understand it, and learn from it.

Once you have prepared yourself for the role of mentor, assessed your skill comfort level, and considered your roles, it is time to prepare the relationship.

Preparing the Relationship

Relationship is the glue of the mentoring partnership. Without it, there is no partnership. Co-preparation of the mentoring partners fosters understanding and clarifies expectations of how the work is going to be done. Some mentees are better prepared to take an active role than others. Mentors may need to apply their own know-how to engage their mentoring partner in the preparation of the relationship. They will need to lay the groundwork to establish, build, and sustain an effective and mutually satisfying relationship by

- Engaging the mentee
- Making the connection
- Checking assumptions

Engaging the Mentee

Mentors who involve mentees in the very first conversation set a positive tone and expectation for active engagement for the entire relationship. The approaches that follow are helpful ways to engage the mentee in initial conversations and throughout the rest of the mentoring relationship.

Satisfying Information Needs

A mentee may have information needs about the subtleties of a particular situation, organization, or office. He or she may want to know the ins and outs of how to scale the corporate walls, publish an article, establish academic credibility, or land that much-sought-after promotion.

Helpful Approaches

- Start with your mentee's questions.
- Identify the mentee's goals.
- Determine what the mentee wants to know.
- Present alternative approaches for reaching the goals.

Not Helpful

- Telling everything there is to know about a subject
- Pontificating
- Talking about "how it was in my day"

Providing Vision

Sometimes all it takes is another perspective to help a mentee reframe learning goals and objectives and create a vision of one's own. Sharing perspectives can broaden the mentee's vision and understanding.

Helpful Approaches

- Ask the obvious and the not so obvious.
- Provide potential alternatives—for example, "Have you thought about . . . ?"
- Provide information about similar other situations—for example, "In my experience . . ."
- Push the mentee's thinking and acting forward by helping in the problem-solving process, not by providing solutions.
- Encourage the exploration of options before pushing to action.

Not Helpful

- Answers
- Demanding that the mentee do things your way

Lending an Ear

Hearing is easy. Really listening to what is being said is not. Yet both are necessary in a meaningful mentoring relationship. Sometimes we fixate on one particular aspect of what we listen to. It could be the words or what someone has said (thinking), the meaning assigned to it (their emotion), or how the person is behaving (tone of voice, facial expressions) as they interact. These affect not only what we listen for but also what it is we actually hear and learn. Hearing means listening for understanding and taking the time to check out what it is you think you heard.

Helpful Approaches

- Suspend judgment.
- Acknowledge emotion.
- Be empathetic.
- Provide feedback appropriately.
- Acknowledge what you hear as well as what is missing from the conversation.

Not Helpful

- Playing therapist
- Concentrating primarily on the mentee's emotions
- Solving the problem for the mentee

Setting Realistic Expectations

When difficulties arise, mentees find someone whose experience and expertise they trust and respect to learn from. But sometimes they lean too hard and expect too much support. An open discussion of realistic expectations and roles can release tension and pressure in the relationship.

Helpful Approaches

- Discourage moaning, groaning, and bemoaning.
- Balance compassion with challenge.
- Ask questions.

Not Helpful

- Becoming a permanent leaning post
- Thinking you are the only one who can help
- Interfering

Establishing the Big Picture

There are layers of complexity to solving business problems. Helping a mentee reach out from the immediate situation to embrace a larger context establishes a broader understanding of a problem, issue, or challenge. Establishing the big picture is often the first step to real understanding.

Helpful Approaches

- Encourage the exploration of options before pushing to action.
- Remember that the complex is often simple.

Not Helpful

- Making seemingly impossible tasks too achievable
- Making it happen

Furnishing a Helping Hand

Sometimes a helping hand provided at just the right time becomes the catalyst to promote a fuller discussion.

Helpful Approaches

- Provide encouragement in multiple and timely ways.
- Know when to ask the right question and how to convey the message, "You can do it."
- Tell your mentee what you are doing and why.
- Talk through possible strategies.
- Co-create opportunities.

Not Helpful

- Scripting for the mentee
- Talking for the mentee or about the mentee in the mentee's presence

Engaging the mentee starts before the relationship is formalized and continues for the duration of the relationship. Each of the strategies set out here for engaging the mentee is useful throughout the mentoring relationship. They are also useful in preliminary discussions with prospective mentees.

Making the Connection

A mentoring relationship without connection is superficial at best. The old notion of mentoring was not concerned with connection as much as it was with the transfer of knowledge and know-how. The distinction between connection and transfer of knowledge and know-how illustrates the difference between separate and connected knowing (Belenky, Clinchy, Goldberger, and Tarule, 1986). Connected knowing emerges out of a relationship between self and other. Transfer of knowledge represents a more impersonal and autonomous way of knowing. We now know that for learning to be effectively sustained, two conditions need to occur: the learner needs to be engaged in the learning process, and the learning needs to be connected to the learner and to his or her life experiences.

Managing expectations in a relationship is difficult when mentoring partners operate under differing assumptions. Examining assumptions prepares the relationship by establishing a connection and managing expectations. Checking out assumptions establishes the basis for candid communication, builds trust, and enables the partners to reach shared understanding, all necessary and vital components of a mentoring relationship. Without shared understanding, trust can quickly erode. Authentic communication is difficult without trust; facilitating learning without it is impossible.

Assumption Awareness

Mentors must be aware of the assumptions they have about mentoring and check regularly to make sure they are valid and accurate (Brookfield, 1995). Brookfield coined the term *assumption hunting* to describe the ethical stance for facilitating learning. Challenging assumptions is part of the learning process. It is also one of the most formidable ethical and caring tasks that mentors carry out. "In many ways," Brookfield writes, "we are our assumptions. Assumptions give meaning and purpose to who we are and what we do. Becoming aware of the implicit assumptions that frame how we think and act is one of the most challenging intellectual puzzles we face in our lives" (p. 2).

Assumption hunting is difficult and challenging work. "When something is considered normal it is woven into our assumptions" (Bardwick, 1998, p. 10) and thus becomes difficult to challenge. We all have our unique definition of what is normal in a mentoring relationship. Sharing those assumptions is a discipline that prepares us for mentoring in an honest, forthright way. Otherwise, existing assumptions guide our actions and get reinforced.

Assumption hunting is vital to improving mentoring relationships and yet can be a daunting task because our assumptions determine how and what we perceive. This means that we ought to engage ourselves in thoughtful reflection about why we do what we do and ask ourselves, "What is it we say to ourselves or to others to justify our actions?"

When Meg took on the role of mentor to Claude, a nurse practitioner, she made the following assumptions:

- That her role was to identify career and educational options that would move him out of his current job into one with more interesting challenges

- That she would need to coach, cheerlead, and help Claude evaluate options

- That her responsibilities would include meeting with Claude once a month, staying connected through e-mail, and making introductions for him

- That Claude would come to the relationship with some ideas about his career options, would follow up on the contacts she provided for him, and would do research between mentoring sessions

- That the mentoring relationship would take about an hour a month face-to-face contact time and that Claude could reach his goals within six months

The Assumption-Hunting Process

The example of Meg and Claude illustrates the first step in the three-step approach to assumption hunting.

Step One: Identify the assumptions you hold about mentoring using the form provided in Exercise 4.7. Complete each box candidly, without any editing.

Step Two: Check your assumptions for validity by asking for feedback from others. If you are participating in a formal or organizational program, you might check with the coordinator and your mentee. If you are engaged in an informal relationship, you might invite your mentee to complete a parallel exercise and share your own responses and discuss the implications for your relationship. This is a helpful exercise for new *and* seasoned mentors. The assumptions you made in previous relationships may not be consistent across relationships.

Meg was surprised to find when she checked in with Claude that he held a different set of assumptions about his role. He had anticipated that Meg would play a more active role in the relationship: setting up interviews for him, coaching him through the interview process, and advocating for him. He was also surprised that Meg had assumed that they would meet

EXERCISE 4.7

Assumption Hunting

Instructions: List the beliefs that you hold regarding each of the following four topics.

My role as mentor

My responsibilities as a mentor

My mentee's role

The mentoring relationship

so infrequently. Holding a discussion about the differences in their assumptions helped them both manage their expectations before they rose to the problem level.

Step Three: Make a habit of checking out your assumptions regularly. You can do this in conversation or by using the guidelines that follow.

Let us assume that Meg and Claude agreed on expectations, but later in the relationship, Claude became increasingly dependent on her for direction. Meg could facilitate a discussion about his assumptions using a similar but more structured approach than the one described in Step Two. She would begin by suggesting that they both list their assumptions about how the relationship was going, share their responses without judging or analyzing them, and then discuss these points:

- What can we conclude based on these assumptions?
- Are our assumptions congruent? If so, on what items? If there is no agreement, why not?
- What are the implications for our learning relationship?
- Where are we likely to encounter choppy water? Smooth sailing?

Assumption Hunting at Work

When assumption hunting is carried out consistently, it enriches the mentoring process. It should be part of the beginning of a mentoring relationship, and surface when evaluating progress in the relationship or when the relationship falls into a rut. Assumption hunting helps raise awareness about why we do things. Examining the congruence between our beliefs and actions helps build and maintain ethically strong mentoring relationships. No mentoring partner is well served by a mentoring relationship based on misunderstanding, which only adds additional layers of vulnerability to the relationship.

Engaging the learner in meaningful conversation from the very beginning starts building the connection, assists in determining the compatibility of goals, and helps a mentee decide whether the mentoring relationship is worth pursuing. Regardless what that decision is, the learning has been facilitated.

Prospecting: Initial Conversations

The natural tendency is to look for chemistry when meeting a prospective mentoring partner. A word of caution is necessary here. Despite the fact that chemistry is one of the first things that prospective mentees look for in a mentoring relationship, chemistry is overrated. If the chemistry does not feel right, the inclination is to shut down or foreclose the opportunity for further engagement. But instead of giving up if the chemistry does not feel right at the first meeting, mentors should ask themselves, "Can I work productively with this individual? Do I honestly feel that I can further this person's learning?"

The initial prospecting conversation includes more than a litmus test for chemistry. It should be used to gauge interest, understand motivation, and check for understanding. Exhibit 4.2 presents strategies and considerations for that initial conversation. During that initial conversation you will want to use the approaches discussed above for engaging the prospective mentee.

It may not be clear from the first conversation or even the second if this mentoring match will make a good partnership for you. The questions in Exercise 4.8 may be helpful in making that decision and also in deciding if you are ready to move on to the next phase of the mentoring relationship.

If you find that there are items that you have not checked, it may mean that you have more work to do to prepare yourself adequately for the partnership, that you may need to have further conversations with your prospective mentee and delay your decision, or that you may decide that you are not ready for this relationship.

The ROS tool (Exercise 3.1) provides a means to test relationship readiness with your mentoring partner before you move onto the negotiating phase. Complete the third matrix column for "Preparing." If you and your mentoring partner can complete it to your satisfaction, then you are ready to begin the negotiating phase. Otherwise continue the conversation until you and your partner reach a comfort level where you can determine if the relationship is ready, the opportunities are ripe, and support for the relationship is in place.

A Final Note

It takes at least two to build a mentoring relationship. This chapter addresses the preparation needs of the mentor and the mentoring relationship. It does not discuss mentee readiness and preparation, which is equally important but is addressed abundantly in the mentoring literature.

Quality preparation directly affects the development and growth of the relationship. By focusing attention on mentor motivation, determining readiness, and assessing comfort with basic mentoring skills, mentor readiness is heightened. Creating readiness helps mentors check out their assumptions, delimit their role, identify and address the skills they want to develop to increase their capacity to mentor well, and determine mentoring fit—all of which ultimately contribute to the mentor's adeptness in facilitating effective learning relationships.

EXHIBIT 4.2

Strategies and Considerations for Initial Conversations

To-Do List	Strategies for Conversation	Mentor Considerations
Take time getting to know each other.	Obtain a copy of the mentee's bio in advance of the conversation. If one is not available, create one through conversation.	Establish rapport. Exchange information. Identify points of connection.
Talk about mentoring.	Ask: Have you ever before been engaged in a mentoring relationship? What did you learn from that experience?	Talk about your own mentoring experiences.
Determine the mentee's goals.	Ask: What do want to learn from this experience? Give the mentee an opportunity to articulate broad goals.	Determine if the mentee is clear about his or her own goals and objectives.
Determine the mentee's relationship needs and expectations.	Ask: What do you want out of the relationship?	Be sure you are clear about what your mentee needs or wants from this mentoring relationship. If you are not, encourage the mentee to think through what he or she wants from the relationship.
Define the deliverables.	Ask: What would success look like for you?	Do you have an area of experience or expertise that is relevant to this person's learning goals?
Share your assumptions, needs, expectations, and limitations candidly.	Ask for feedback. Discuss: Implications for relationship.	What you are willing and capable of contributing to the relationship?
Discuss options and opportunities for learning.	Ask: How would you like to go about achieving your learning goals? Discuss ways: learning and communication styles Ask: What is the most useful kind of assistance I can provide? Discuss means: Shadowing, project?	Discuss implications of each other's styles and how that might affect the relationship.

EXERCISE 4.8

Preparing: A Readiness Checklist

Instructions: Review the list below, and check all items that apply to you with respect to your prospective mentoring relationship.

1. ____   I have a sincere interest in helping this person succeed.

2. ____   There appears to be mutual interest and compatibility.

3. ____   Our assumptions about the process are congruent.

4. ____   I am clear about my role.

5. ____   I am the right person to help achieve these goals.

6. ____   I can enthusiastically engage in helping this person.

7. ____   I am willing to use my network of contacts to help this individual.

8. ____   I can commit adequate time to mentoring this person.

9. ____   I have access to the kind of opportunities that can support this person's learning.

10. ____   I have the support that I need to be able to engage in this relationship in a meaningful way.

11. ____   I am committed to developing my own mentoring skills.

12. ____   I have a mentoring development plan in place.

CHAPTER 5

Planting Seeds

Negotiating

Weave real connections, create real nodes, build real houses.
—MARGE PIERCY, "The Seven of Pentacles"

The negotiating phase is a process of conversation, consensus, and commitment. Partners engage in conversation (weave real connections) about how the learning process will unfold (create real nodes) and what outcomes they want to achieve during the relationship (build real houses). Depth, specificity, and framework are added to the broad goals identified during the preparing phase. The outcome of this phase is a mentoring partnership work plan anchored in well-defined goals, measurements for success, delineation of mutual responsibility, accountability mechanisms, and protocols for dealing with stumbling blocks.

Negotiating describes a free-flowing focused conversational process that takes place over one or several sessions and results in a shared understanding about the outcome and process of the mentoring partnership. The defining question in the negotiating conversation is How will our work move forward? Ultimately the answer depends on the willingness of mentoring partners to invest adequate time and effort into a thoughtful negotiating conversation—one that anticipates pitfalls, allows for the exploration of emerging possibilities and alternate pathways, and accommodates renegotiations or closure should they become necessary or prudent. A good mentoring negotiation process will result in the following:

- Well-defined goals
- Success criteria and measurement
- Delineation of mutual responsibilities
- Accountability assurances
- Protocols for addressing stumbling blocks
- A consensual mentoring agreement.
- A work plan for achieving learning goals

Exhibit 5.1 lists each outcome and the questions that need to be answered in order to achieve it.

The negotiating phase plants the seeds that make it possible for the relationship to bud and flower. This chapter details the content agenda of the negotiating conversation needed to achieve the outcomes.

Developing an Agreement

A mentoring partnership agreement resembles a learning contract and is consistent with sound principles and practices of adult learning. Like a learning contract, it is an agreement between parties (in the case of a learning contract, an instructor and a learner) that articulates specific components of the learning agreement: objectives, evidence of accomplishment of objectives, learning resources and strategies, criteria, and the means for validating the learning (Knowles, 1980). Just as learning contracts are beneficial in setting up boundaries and containing expectations (Galbraith, 1991), so too are mentoring partnership agreements.

The conversation that takes place in the process of developing mentoring agreement sows the seeds of the relationship to follow. A mentoring agreement arrived at without conversation is a missed opportunity for connection. Each of the following sections lays out the areas for discussion in arriving at an agreement.

Well-Defined Goals

There is nothing quite as important as having well-defined learning goals in a mentoring relationship. Since learning is the quintessential purpose of the relationship, all that follows depends on clearly defining desired learning goals. Clarifying and articulating learning goals is indispensable to the work of negotiating the mentoring relationship. Mentoring partners continuously revisit their learning goals throughout the mentoring relationship.

EXHIBIT 5.1

Mentoring Negotiating Questions and Outcomes

Outcomes	Questions Answered
Well-defined goals	• What are the specific learning outcomes desired from this relationship?
Success criteria and measurement	• What are the criteria for evaluating successful accomplishment of learning outcomes? • What is the process for evaluating success?
Delineation of mutual responsibility	• Who will be responsible for what?
Accountability assurances	• How do we ensure we do what we say we are going to do?
Relationship ground rules	• What are the norms and guidelines we will follow in conducting the relationship?
Confidentiality safeguards	• How do we protect the confidentiality of this relationship?
Boundaries	• What are the not-to-exceed limits of this relationship?
Protocols for addressing stumbling blocks	• What stumbling blocks might we encounter? • What process should we have in place to deal with them as they occur?
Consensual mentoring agreement	• What do we need to include to make this agreement work for us?
A work plan for achieving learning goals	• What is the process? • What are the steps for achieving the goals?

It is hard to achieve a goal if it has not been defined. Without well-defined goals, the relationship runs the risk of losing its focus. Lack of clarity leads to diffusion of effort, as this female mentor from a social service agency recalls: "I probably wasn't as clear as I should have been about insisting we have specific goals. We really didn't sit down and talk about goals. I didn't know that goals were an important part."

Specificity is an important part of clarity. Many mentoring relationships never get beyond a broad goal definition. Another mentor, a male manager, described a similar experience: "We were not really clear about the goals despite the fact that we had talked about it up front. We should have been more specific and concrete. Lack of it made our relationship a meandering process that was not as helpful as it could have been to each of us."

Some mentees come to a mentoring relationship with well-defined goals. Nevertheless, it is still important when this is the case for mentors to check out their assumptions regarding the goals and determine if there is a good fit between the mentee's desired learning outcome and their own experience and expertise.

When mentees do not have well-defined goals, goal setting becomes the first priority, and the mentor's immediate task is to assist the mentee in clarifying and defining goals. This must be completed before the work phase of the relationship begins.

Goal setting is an evolutionary process that takes time. The process usually begins as a fairly broad statement of intent—from the general (in the preparing phase) to the more specific (in the negotiating phase). If goals are left too broad, chances are that neither the mentor nor the mentee will be satisfied with the learning process, the learning outcome, or the mentoring relationship. Because the length of a mentoring relationship, and particularly an informal relationship, is at least in part determined by the accomplishment of desired learning goals, establishing well-defined goals is critical.

Most mentees come to mentoring with an idea about what they want to learn. That idea becomes the starting point for providing assistance in the goal-setting process. There are a number of ways that mentors can help mentees develop concrete, concise, and clear goals.

When mentors encourage a mentee to put goals in writing, they encourage specificity. Once goals are defined in writing, they can be used as an accountability tool to benchmark progress. Well-defined goals are like the mission statement of the relationship; they maintain the focus of the relationship and keep it on track.

Smith (1995) identifies five criteria for creating "SMART" goals: goals must be specific (S), measurable (M), action oriented (A), realistic (R), and timely (T). Exercise 5.1 is a worksheet for mentors to complete to assess how well mentee goals are defined. The worksheet can also be completed by the mentor and mentee as a prelude to developing the components of the mentoring partnership agreement. Exhibit 5.2 shows a completed worksheet. This mentor quickly realized that the mentee's goals were not well defined and that there was more work to be done before moving forward.

Well-defined goals help identify the deliverables—the measures for success. As circumstances change over the course of the relationship, goals may need to be reformulated.

Success Criteria and Measurement

For the success of the learning effort to be measured, criteria for the accomplishment of learning outcomes must be defined. These criteria are the deliverables or intended learning results, and they flow directly from the goals. When mentoring partners engage in a conversation around the topic of how they will know when they achieve their goals, they are defining their deliverables. Once the goal is well defined, it is an easy conversation. The example in Exhibit 5.2 shows that this mentoring partnership is not yet ready to decide on criteria.

Once the criteria for success have been identified, the next step is to think about how success will be measured, that is, what the process is for evaluating success. In many instances, the process is readily apparent. In some, the answer to that question may need time. This is because learning often comes from application and integration, long after the mentoring relationship has concluded.

Delineation of Mutual Responsibility

Being a mentor is a commitment and therefore involves responsibilities. In any viable partnership, the responsibilities of each partner should be defined and mutually understood. This is the only way there can be meaningful accountability.

Mentors must be clear about their own responsibilities as well as those of their mentoring partner. Mentors who are in a formal mentoring program can begin with a review of the mentor's job description and discuss the implications for their particular relationship with their mentoring partner. For example, John's accounting firm has an internal mentoring program to

EXERCISE 5.1

Mentor's Worksheet for Evaluating Mentee Goals

Instructions: Answer the following questions to gauge the clarity of your mentee's goals.

Specific

- What is it the mentee is trying to accomplish in this relationship?

- Are the mentee's goals specific, concrete, and clear?

Measurable

- Are the goals capable of being measured?

- In what ways can success be measured?

Action Oriented

- Are the goals future oriented?

- What results should you be able to see when the mentee's goals are accomplished?

- What concrete things will the mentee be able to do as a result of accomplishing the goals identified?

Realistic

- Are goals achievable within the availability of your time?

- Are there other resources that need to be available in order to achieve the goals?

Timely

- Is the time allocated for accomplishing the learning goals reasonable?

- Has a completion date been set for attaining the goals?

Source: Adapted from Smith (1995, pp. 83–84).

EXHIBIT 5.2

Completed Mentor's Worksheet for Evaluating Mentee Goals

Stated Goal: To seek assistance in finding a job situation in the next 12 to 18 months that will pay more, have opportunities for growth, and be closer to my family.

Specific: What is it the mentee is trying to accomplish in this relationship? Are the mentee's goals specific, concrete, and clear?

Mentee states that she wants to find a situation where she can better balance work and family life. Her mother is becoming increasingly infirm, and she states she needs to earn more, take on more responsibility at work, and be closer to her mom.

Things I would like to know: What does "pay more" mean? What kind of opportunities for growth is she looking for? Is she talking about career advancement? Knowledge enhancement?

Measurable: Are the goals capable being of measured? In what ways can success be measured?

Certainly will know more about this once I have a clearer idea of the answers to question above.

Success can be measured easily once she puts the dollar sign on. Distance is readily measured. In terms of career advancement, I need to know what her goals are and what her definition is for those terms.

Action Oriented: Are the goals future oriented? What results should you be able to see when the mentee's goals are accomplished? What concrete things will the mentee be able to do as a result of accomplishing the goals identified?

No problem here. I should be able to see a woman who is feeling more balanced, satisfied, and enthusiastic about her work and less guilty about the geographic distance. Eventually she will be ready to move. When she does, hopefully she will learn a way of thinking about career development from an ongoing growth perspective.

Realistic: Are goals achievable within the availability of your time? Are there other resources necessary in order to achieve the goals?

I see my job as guiding her through the process. Initially our time will be spent in getting more clarity on this opportunity thing. She is going to have to find time to do a lot of the investigative work herself. I can set her on the right course, but she will have lots of decisions ahead of her. She is going to work on defining the career advancement piece.

She may need to go to a career placement agency, recruitment agency, or similar companies to get access to some of the resources she will need. She will need to get on-line and stay on-line, and do plenty of networking.

Timely: Is the time allocated for accomplishing learning goals reasonable? Has a completion date been set for attainment of the goals?

Yes, assuming she is willing to dedicate time and energy to the task. She has laid out a framework in broad brush strokes. I will want to urge her to be more specific when we see how things develop.

orient new employees to the firm's culture and business practices. The program also is intended to contribute to individual skill development and competency development. The mentor's responsibilities include providing support, guidance, and hands-on opportunities for the mentee to learn. It is also the mentor's responsibility to provide specific feedback to the mentee and ongoing programmatic feedback to the mentoring program oversight committee. Mentors must attend training sessions twice a year and meet regularly with mentees—at least twice a week for the first month, once a week for the next five months, and twice monthly for one year after the date of hire.

John's mentee has a list of responsibilities as well. Among them are participating as an active learner in the relationship, attending a mentoring orientation program, agreeing to the protocols outlined in the mentoring program, honoring the confidentiality of their conversations, and providing feedback to the mentor and the program oversight committee.

There are less visible partners involved in the mentoring relationship as well. These partners may include the mentee's manager, the program supervisor, and the human resource specialist. Each of these individuals has responsibilities affecting the relationship directly or indirectly. Being aware of those responsibilities militates against the problem of role diffusion.

Linda is engaged in an informal mentoring relationship. Her goal as a mentee is to learn everything she can about becoming an editor. She is new to her position as managing editor and chose to go outside the company for mentoring assistance. Although she writes well, Linda has never been a managing editor before and has a need to learn quickly so that she can make a positive impression on subscribers, advertisers, and her staff. Gerald, her mentor, has agreed to share his experiences and meet with her on a regular basis, but he is unwilling to accept the responsibility for scheduling their appointments and keeping her on task. They agree that it is Linda's responsibility to bring the problems, situations, and questions she has to the relationship. Gerald has accepted responsibility for getting her connected with some professional associations. They agree to accept mutual responsibility for evaluating Linda's progress every other month.

Defining responsibilities is essential if there is to be any level of meaningful accountability in a relationship.

Accountability Assurances

Accountability is the conscious melding of self-responsibility and rigor. Accountability assurance is based on considered commitment to and clear understanding of the responsibilities of each mentoring partner. The defining accountability question is, How are we going to hold ourselves and each other accountable in this mentoring relationship? Answering the question calls for clarity—the kind of clarity that Patrick Lencioni writes about in *The Five Temptations of a CEO* (1998), where he states, "You can't hold people accountable for things that aren't clear" (p. 51).

Those who are engaged in an informal mentoring relationship may view an imposed accountability procedure as cumbersome. However, unless external accountability measures are built in, whether self or other imposed, the temptation is to sidestep it altogether. The accountability conversation provides a touchstone for the relationship. When used thoughtfully, it becomes an ongoing quality assurance conversation.

There are three levels of accountability that mentoring partners ought to address: accountability for the relationship, accountability for the learning process, and the accountability for the achievement of the learning goals. Exhibit 5.3 provides some prototypical questions associated with each level.

As you think about meeting the challenge of mutual accountability in a mentoring relationship, consider how best to encourage and support accountability.

Encouraging Accountability

Accountability conversations do not have to be formal, but they do need to be meaningful and regular. Periodically asking, "How is it going?" keeps accountability at the forefront. Posing a simple question regularly instead of waiting until something goes amiss offers a nonthreatening approach. When checking in is an established, normative part of the relationship, it takes the pressure off and encourages accountability.

In some situations, more detailed accountability mechanisms are appropriate. If this is not the case, the mentor and mentee could choose to develop a list of itemized questions to discuss at predefined milestones in the relationship.

Supporting Accountability

The responsibility for accountability rests with the mentoring partners. Some mentors suggest that mentees summarize the mentoring session at the close of the interaction and record what they have learned. At the beginning of the next session, mentees review that summary. This ensures continuity and a jumping-off point for talking about progress made since the previous mentoring session or conversation. Other mentors make process notes for themselves and continue to add to them and review them throughout the

Exhibit 5.3

Levels of Ongoing Accountability

The relationship	How are we doing?
	What is the quality of our interaction?
	In what ways might we strengthen our relationship?
The learning process	Is the process we are using working to facilitate your learning?
	In what ways are your learning needs being met? Not met?
	What might we do to make the process work better for you? What do we need to change or strengthen?
	What are you learning about yourself as a learner in this process?
Progress toward learning goals	What progress are you making toward realizing your learning goals?
	What is your greatest success thus far?
	What is your biggest frustration?
	What gives you the most satisfaction about what you are learning?

mentoring relationship. This is particularly helpful when mentoring at a distance or when there is time distance between mentoring interactions. By saving these notes, each partner has a record of the mentoring journey that becomes a helpful point of departure in assessing the learning experience.

Group mentoring situations offer a unique opportunity for supporting accountability. Using a round-robin approach to summarize and end the session both reinforces the learning and reminds mentees of what they need to do. Beginning the next session with a progress report since the previous session helps focus the interaction and abbreviate start-up time.

E-mail or handwritten notes, sharing an interesting article, and a quick telephone call are little ways of supporting accountability.

Critical Aspects of Accountability

Three aspects of accountability are critical to mutual accountability for building and maintaining the relationship: ground rules, confidentiality safeguards, and boundary setting.

Ground Rules for the Relationship We sometimes take partnering for granted and assume that it will happen naturally. This assumption often undermines the relationship. Establishing ground rules helps manage expectations in a mentoring relationship.

Ground rules are the norms or accepted behaviors, rules of the road, guidelines, or conventions that partners agree to abide by in a partnership. They should not restrict the relationship, but rather encourage and support accountability. At a minimum, a mentoring partnership agreement should outline the norms of the relationship.

The following common mentoring norms can be used to start the discussion on ground rules:

- Our meetings begin and end on time.

- Each of us actively participates in the relationship.

- Our communication is open, candid, and direct.

- We will respect our differences and learn from them.

- We will honor each other's expertise and experience.

- We will safeguard confidentiality.

- We will manage our time well.

- We will put interruptions aside.

The most challenging part of the ground rule conversation is the discussion about what happens if and when these rules are not followed. What will happen if one partner dominates the relationship? What are the sanctions if appointment times are not honored? What happens when confidentiality is compromised? In a formal mentoring situation, there may be additional programmatic sanctions imposed that will need to be taken into consideration.

Checking in to determine whether the ground rules are working effectively at the beginning or end of the first several mentoring sessions helps smooth the way and avoid difficulties later on. Whatever both partners ultimately decide about the ground rules of their mentoring partnership, they should consider establishing checkpoints to monitor the status of the relationship and agree in advance on what those will be.

Confidentiality Safeguards Breach of confidentiality is a major stumbling block in mentoring relationships. Although mentees often confide in mentors and mentors in mentees, many people have differing expectations of what that confidentiality means. Being a confidant does not always mean that person you trust automatically safeguards confidentiality the way you would.

Generally people do not like to talk about confidentiality; they just assume it. And because they assume it, assumptions remain undisclosed and untested. Instead, mentors and mentees must continuously check out their own assumptions if they are to share mutual accountability for the mentoring partnership.

It is hard to talk about confidentiality because people are afraid it will undermine trust and fear a conversation about it will be offensive. They see confidentiality as a particularly difficult issue to discuss when there appears to be no immediate reason to do so.

The truth of the matter is that there are many different expectations about what confidentiality means in a relationship. Some people view confidential information as private, restricted, secret, undisclosed, and classified. For others, confidentiality has a limited duration. It is important to talk candidly with mentees and agree on every aspect of confidentiality in a mentoring relationship.

Getting the conversation about confidentiality started is sometimes awkward. We examine two possible approaches that can be used independent of each other or in combination to frame the conversation: perception identification and assumption testing.

In perception identification, the mentor and mentee begin the discussion of confidentiality using a free association exercise. They individually write down words associated with the word *confidentiality*, thereby generating a list that can serve as a basis for discussion. Ultimately the partners will come to mutual agreement about what confidentiality will mean in their relationship.

Assumption testing can be accomplished using Exercise 5.2, which lists eight common assumptions about confidentiality. The mentor and mentee should review the list independently to establish a framework for candidly discussing their own assumptions about confidentiality. The discussion of their responses encourages additional assumptions to emerge. Working from this prepared list focuses the conversation and makes discussion of this slippery concept much less threatening.

There must be clarity about what confidentiality means within a particular mentoring relationship. The object is to create consensus about what

EXERCISE 5.2

Checklist for Assumption Testing About Confidentiality

Instructions: Answer each question with "yes," "no," or "not sure." Make copies of this checklist before you complete it. Complete a copy yourself, and ask your mentee to complete a copy. When you have completed all eight items, decide whether there are other assumptions that you hold that should be added to the list. Review and discuss each item with your mentee. Allow for a full discussion of gaps before coming to consensus.

Which of the following assumptions about confidentiality do you hold?

_____ 1. What we discuss stays between us for as long as we are engaged in our mentoring relationship.

_____ 2. If asked by your supervisor, I can freely disclose our conversation.

_____ 3. After our formal mentoring relationship has ended, it is okay to talk about what we discussed or how we related.

_____ 4. If there is a demonstrated need to know, I can appropriately disclose our conversations, my impressions, or anything else that pertains to the relationship.

_____ 5. What we say between us stays there unless you give me permission to talk about it with others.

_____ 6. Some issues will be kept confidential, while others will not.

_____ 7. It is okay to discuss how we relate to one another but not the content of our discussions.

_____ 8. It is okay to talk about what we talk about as long as it is positive.

Are there other assumptions I hold that should be added to this list?

is confidential and what is not that makes sense for the mentoring partners and promotes open and candid communication—communication that is authentic and free flowing—without getting so specific that conversation is restricted, unnatural, and guarded. Delimiting confidentiality is part of the boundary-setting process and helps ensure accountability within the relationship.

Boundary Setting   A frank discussion about the limits and boundaries of the mentoring relationship enables mentoring partners to sustain the focus on learning, manage expectations, and ensure mutual accountability throughout the duration of the relationship. Boundaries that go undefined frequently undermine the relationship by deflecting energy away from the learning focus of the relationship. When boundaries are too loose, they may be misinterpreted, and when they are too rigid, they incapacitate the relationship.

Boundaries are not always clear-cut, however, and may vary according to circumstance. There are boundaries that we set for ourselves and boundaries that we set in partnership with others. There are boundaries that are evident at the beginning of the relationship and boundaries that need to be set during the relationship. Personal boundary setting during the negotiating phase helps mentors maintain the delicate balance between meeting their own needs and those of their mentees.

Dora saw great promise in Theo and wanted to see him succeed as quickly as possible. She encouraged him to stop into her office whenever he had a question. Before long, answering Theo's interruptions was taking up a significant portion of Dora's work time, and she was falling behind in meeting department deadlines. The push and pull she was experiencing was the result of not having set personal boundaries and failing to communicate those boundaries to her mentee.

The most overlooked aspect of boundary setting has to do with access, which directly relates to managing expectations:

What kind of access does the mentee have to you?

What is the limit?

Does being a mentor mean the mentee has unlimited access to you for the duration of the relationship?

Is an appointment needed?

What kind of telephone access does the mentee have to you?

Will your mentee need to go through a gatekeeper to get to you?

It is important for mentors to communicate what they are willing to do and unwilling to do in the relationship. Once they become aware of their own boundaries, the next step is to decide what they expect from the mentee to respect these boundaries. A list of boundaries can be used as a basis for conversation with the mentee at the appropriate time in the negotiating process.

Mentees also need to set boundaries for themselves. Maria was so anxious to please her mentor that she volunteered time to help her mentor and did whatever was asked of her. Soon her mentor came to expect that level of performance from her. The ante was raised, and Maria felt there was nothing she could do. She had allowed her mentoring relationship to encroach on the rest of her life.

Relationship boundary setting requires a discussion about the boundaries of the relationship. Guidelines for safeguarding confidentiality are an example of a partnership boundary. Guidelines for maintaining contact are another. Access is yet another.

Despite best intentions, boundaries are crossed and limits are exceeded. Crossing boundaries affects the mentoring relationship and the learning taking place within it. The best way to handle this is to be prepared with a strategy to deal with boundary crossing if and when it occurs. Exhibit 5.4 presents some potential strategies to consider when boundaries are crossed.

Protocols for Addressing Stumbling Blocks

Even with accountability assurances in place, most relationships encounter stumbling blocks at one time or another. There are two steps that can prepare mentoring partners to address issues before they rise to the level of stumbling block: mutually anticipate what the stumbling blocks might be and discuss procedures to follow when stumbling blocks do occur.

To anticipate what stumbling blocks might occur, the partners can envision and talk about what internal and external factors might affect the relationship. For example, the birth of a child, the imminent death of a loved one, pressures at work, a job change, or a sabbatical could all create stumbling blocks. Once these are identified, mentor and mentee can determine how to deal with them when they do occur.

Closure, for example, is a potential stumbling block for most relationships. Both mentor and mentee must agree how they will end the mentoring relationship when that time eventually arrives. Successful closure depends on having well-defined goals as well as the opportunity for high-level closure conversation that engages the partners in processing the learning, the learning experience, and the accomplishments. It is important to predefine

EXHIBIT 5.4

Responses to Crossed Boundaries

Boundary Crossed	What to Do
Mentee demands more time than the mentor is willing to give.	Mentees should not "demand" anything. This is a partnership. If more time is needed, the mentoring partnership agreement should be revisited.
Mentee misses scheduled meetings and does not call to explain.	Mentoring is a partnership built on respect for the individual. This includes respect for the mentor's time. You may need to renegotiate the mentoring agreement.
Mentee starts confiding serious personal problems.	Avoid playing therapist. The mentor-mentee relationship focuses on fulfilling learning needs, not psychological needs.
Mentee calls too frequently for advice.	Mentor and mentee need to talk about why this is happening and review the mentoring partnership agreement.

the terms of the closure to the extent that you can. If you are participating in a mentoring program, likely these will be defined in part for you.

Not all stumbling blocks are predictable, however. Thus, the second step is to discuss procedures or protocols to deal with stumbling blocks when they occur. Mapping out protocols is an important step in keeping the lines of communication open. For example, one of the major stumbling blocks is erosion of boundaries. Mentoring partners might agree to the following procedures when boundaries are crossed:

- Let your mentoring partner know that a boundary has been crossed.
- Refer to the ground rules outlined in your mentoring agreement.
- Describe the behaviors that clearly demonstrate how the boundary was crossed.
- Request that the behaviors stop.
- If your mentoring partner acknowledges that boundaries have been crossed, let that person know you appreciate the understanding.

- If boundaries go unacknowledged and continue to be crossed, ask your mentoring partner to stop crossing the line. Second, insist that they be stopped. Third, walk away from the relationship.

A Consensual Mentoring Agreement

Putting shared understandings about a partnership in writing facilitates the learning process. The form the mentoring agreement takes is not as important as the contents. The agreement could contain a series of bulleted notes that resulted from the negotiating conversation, a written contract, a memo of understanding, or a learning contract. By mutually choosing a form or format, the agreement becomes meaningful to both partners. You and your mentoring partner may want to use Exercise 5.3 as a template, with the answers to the questions serving as their mentoring agreement. (Exercise 5.4 is a streamlined template.) Exhibit 5.5 contains a sample mentoring partnership agreement that used the template in Exercise 5.3.

The templates may suggest other forms and formats. Whatever the ultimate form the agreement takes, it must be clear to all mentoring partners and emerge from shared understandings. Constructing the agreement together helps ensure this end. It builds trust and creates shared accountability.

The following guidelines pertain to developing the partnership agreement:

- Agree on the goals of the relationship.

- Note the ground rules for the relationship.

- Spell out the "what-ifs": what to do in case time availability becomes an issue, for example, or in case of incompatibility.

- Determine criteria for success and the completion of the relationship.

- Decide how to come to closure if the relationship terminates by mutual consent (or not).

- Establish how to process learnings from the relationship in a learning conclusion.

Whether the end result is a formal or informal agreement, contract, or written set of goals and operating procedures depends entirely on the partners. It may be that a written document is more than is needed; in this situation, a dedicated conversation, with something in writing—say, notes or a journal entry—is highly recommended. "In the final analysis what is right will be what works for you. It must be appropriate to your style, circumstances and way of doing things" (Owen, 1992). The process of formulating a mentoring partnership agreement is as important as the agreement itself.

EXERCISE 5.3

Mentoring Partnership Agreement Template

Instructions: This is a sample of the mentoring partnership agreement. Use this template after completing the negotiating conversations discussed earlier in this chapter.

We have agreed on the following goals and objectives as the focus of this mentoring relationship:

1.

2.

3.

We have discussed the protocols by which we will work together, develop, and, in that same spirit of partnership, collaborate on the development of a work plan. In order to ensure that our relationship is a mutually rewarding and satisfying experience for both of us, we agree to:

1. Meet regularly.

   Our specific schedule of contact and meetings, including additional meetings, is as follows:

2. Look for multiple opportunities and experiences to enhance the mentee's learning.

   We have identified, and will commit to, the following specific opportunities and venues for learning:

3. Maintain confidentiality of our relationship.

   Confidentiality for us means ...

4. Honor the ground rules we have developed for the relationship.

   Our ground rules will be ...

5. Provide regular feedback to each other and evaluate progress. We will accomplish this by ...

We agree to meet regularly until we accomplish our predefined goals or for a maximum of [specify time frame]. At the end of this period of time, we will review this agreement, evaluate our progress, and reach a learning conclusion. The relationship will then be considered complete. If we choose to continue our mentoring partnership, we may negotiate a basis for continuation, so long as we have stipulated mutually agreed-on goals.

In the event one of us believes it is no longer productive for us to continue or the learning situation is compromised, we may decide to seek outside intervention or conclude the relationship. In this event, we agree to use closure as a learning opportunity.

_____   _____
Mentor's Signature and Date   Mentee's Signature and Date

EXERCISE 5.4

Streamlined Mentoring Partnership Agreement Template

Instructions: This is a more streamlined mentoring partnership agreement. Use this template after completing the negotiating conversations presented earlier in this chapter.

Goals:

Learning Outcomes:

Ground Rules:

Parameters for the Relationship:

Steps to Achieving the Goals and Learning Outcomes:

Time Frame:

Checkpoints:

_____   _____
Mentor's Signature and Date   Mentee's Signature and Date

EXHIBIT 5.5

Sample Mentoring Partnership Agreement

We have agreed on the following goals and objectives as the focus of this mentoring relationship:

To develop a leadership career pathway to prepare the mentee to assume a significant high-profile leadership position within the community

To assist mentee in depth analysis of leadership strengths and weaknesses

To create a leadership development plan for mentee

To introduce mentee to best-practice leadership experiences

We have discussed the protocols by which we will work together, develop, and, in that same spirit of partnership, collaborate on the development of a work plan. In order to ensure that our relationship is a mutually rewarding and satisfying experience for both of us, we agree to:

1. Meet regularly.

   Our specific schedule of contact and meetings, including additional meetings, is as follows:

   We will meet twice a month and be in contact by telephone or e-mail at least once a week.

2. Look for multiple opportunities and experiences to enhance the mentee's learning.

   We have identified, and will commit to, the following specific opportunities and venues for learning:

   Mentee will attend board meetings as mentor's guest. We will meet prior to each meeting and debrief following each meeting.

   Mentee will attend a nonprofit institute with mentor.

   Mentee and mentor will attend community leadership forum meetings.

3. Maintain confidentiality of our relationship.

   Confidentiality for us means that what we discuss remains between us. Mentor and mentee will agree ahead of time if specific information is to be shared with anyone else.

4. Honor the ground rules we have developed for the relationship.

   Our ground rules will be: We will meet after business hours. Mentee will assume responsibility for confirming meetings. Mentee will pay for own expenses. Mentee will maintain an ongoing journal of mentoring experience. At the conclusion of each meeting, we will target topics for discussion at the next session.

5. Provide regular feedback to each other and evaluate progress. We will accomplish this by:

   Reviewing learning goals once a month, discussing progress, and checking in with each other regularly for the first month to make sure our individual needs are being met in the relationship, and periodically thereafter.

We agree to meet regularly until we have accomplished our predefined goals or for a maximum of eighteen months. At the end of this period of time, we will review this agreement, evaluate our progress, and reach a learning conclusion. The relationship then will be considered complete. If we choose to continue our mentoring partnership, we may negotiate a basis for continuation, so long as we have stipulated the mutually agreed-on goals.

In the event one of us believes it is no longer productive for us to continue or the learning situation is compromised, we may decide to seek outside intervention or conclude the relationship. In this event we agree to use closure as a learning opportunity.

Mentor's Signature and Date   Mentee's Signature and Date

It plants the seeds for a fruitful relationship.

Once the agreement is negotiated, both mentor and mentee should be clear about the following issues:

- The goals of the relationship
- What the mentee wants to learn
- What the mentee needs from the relationship
- How often the mentor and mentee need to meet
- What kind of learning supports the mentee's needs
- How much time the mentee has committed to achieving the learning goals
- How the mentee prefers to learn
- How the mentor plans to encourage and support accountability

Developing the Work Plan

Once mentoring partners have come to agreement, the next step is to develop an action plan to achieve each of the goals and objectives. Exercise 5.5 offers an approach to developing a partnership work plan:

1. Identify the learning goals.

2. Lay out the objectives, which describe how to achieve the goals. Objectives must be specific and measurable with visible results. A goal might be "expanding my leadership capability so that I can move up the ladder in my company." An objective would be "determining which three new assignments I can take on that would give me the exposure and experience."

3. Identify the learning tasks—the specific steps that need to be taken to meet the objectives. For example, in order to "determine new assignments," what will the mentee have to do? Attend a conference? Take on a project? Shadow the mentor? Make presentations? It is helpful to know something about the mentee's learning style when designing this part of the work plan.

4. List potential resources—both human and material. Examples are interviewing specific individuals and reading several briefing documents.

5. Set a target date. People are more likely to make progress if they are trying to meet a deadline. The partners can always renegotiate the time frame, but setting a date designates a specific time to evaluate progress, assess where the partners are, and determine how the relationship is going to proceed.

EXERCISE 5.5

Mentoring Planning Form

LEARNING GOAL(S)

OBJECTIVES	LEARNING TASKS AND PROCESSES	RESOURCES	TARGET DATE

EXERCISE 5.6

Negotiating: A Readiness Checklist

Instructions: Complete the following checklist to determine if you have sufficiently completed the negotiating phase.

____ 1. Accountabilities are in place for me, my partner, and the relationship.

____ 2. Expectations are clear.

____ 3. Goals are well defined and clear.

____ 4. The responsibilities of each partner are defined.

____ 5. Norms have been developed and agreed to.

____ 6. We have decided how often should we meet.

____ 7. We are in agreement about how often we should connect and who should do the connecting.

____ 8. We have articulated criteria for success.

____ 9. We have developed a workable strategy for dealing with obstacles to the relationship.

____ 10. The work plan makes sense.

____ 11. We have discussed how and when the relationship will be brought to closure.

____ 12. Our operating assumptions about confidentiality are well articulated.

____ 13. The boundaries and limits of this relationship leave enough room for flexibility.

Moving On

When learning permeates the negotiating phase, it is not cumbersome or restrictive. In fact, it is often quite liberating because mentoring partners have a map and a compass to guide them through the remaining phases. A mutual commitment to fulfillment of the mentee's goals enriches the partnership. Mentoring partners stand a better chance of holding each other accountable. Having a formalized mentoring agreement does not preclude having an informal mentoring relationship. Articulating the commitment increases the likelihood of success.

Once mentoring partners come to agreement and articulate a work plan, it is time to begin implementing the plan. The items in Exercise 5.6 provide a checklist to see whether the work of the negotiating phase is complete.

If you were able to complete the checklist in Exercise 5.6, then you are ready to move on to the enabling phase and implement the mentoring partnership agreement. If you could not, it may be a sign that you need to seek clarification and talk further with your mentee until you feel comfortable enough to check all these items affirmatively. You may also find it helpful to revisit the ROS tool (Exercise 3.1) and complete the third matrix column for "Negotiating." If you and your mentoring partner can complete it to your mutual satisfaction, then you are ready to begin the enabling phase.

CHAPTER 6

Nurturing Growth
Enabling

Keep tangling and interweaving and taking more in.
—MARGE PIERCY, "The Seven of Pentacles"

The enabling phase is the linchpin in the learning process. The seeds of the mentoring relationship take root, and the mentee's growth is nurtured as the partners "keep tangling and interweaving and taking more" into the relationship. As they work together, the relationship grows and, hopefully, flourishes, as mentee learning goals are met.

Providing adequate support, appropriate challenge, and ample vision are core conditions that work together to facilitate mentee growth and development, particularly (although not exclusively) throughout the enabling phase. Mentors manage the relationship and support learning by creating a learning environment and building and maintaining the relationship. They maintain momentum by providing appropriate levels of challenge, monitoring the process, and evaluating progress. And they encourage movement by providing vision, fostering reflection, and encouraging personal benchmarking against desired learning outcomes. Exhibit 6.1 illustrates how Daloz's (1999) conditions of support, challenge, and vision relate to the ongoing work of this phase.

This chapter integrates many of the concepts and processes presented in earlier chapters and describes the mentor's key tasks as they relate to each of the three core conditions: support, challenge, and vision.

EXHIBIT 6.1

Nurturing Growth in the Enabling Phase

Conditions That Facilitate Growth and Development[a]	Enabling Process and Functions[b]	Mentor's Key Tasks
Support	**Managing the Process** Listening Providing structure Expressing positive expectations Serving as advocate Sharing ourselves Making it special	• Creating a learning environment • Building and maintaining the relationship
Challenge	**Maintaining Momentum** Setting tasks Engaging in discussion Setting up dichotomies Constructing hypotheses Setting high standards	• Monitoring the process • Evaluating progress
Vision	**Encouraging Movement** Modeling Keeping tradition Offering a map Suggesting new language Providing a mirror	• Fostering reflection • Assessing learning outcomes

[a]See Daloz (1999, Chap. 8) for full description of the facilitative behaviors.

[b]The functions listed in Column 2 are discussed extensively in Daloz (1999) and are not directly explained in this chapter. They are listed here to illustrate the processes a mentor might use to enable mentee learning.

Considerable treatment is given to two strategic enabling processes that permeate the conditions (and transcend the enabling phases): engaging in meaningful feedback and overcoming obstacles. By modeling and coaching mentees in how to ask for, receive, accept, apply, and integrate feedback, mentors honor the adult capacity for self-directed learning. When external and internal obstacles threaten the viability of a mentoring relationship, knowing what to do to overcome them helps keep the relationship focused on its intended purpose: the learning. Ongoing feedback can prevent the very situations that create obstacles to learning.

The example of Ruth and Lorraine helps illustrate how the concepts of support, challenge, and vision work to enable a mentoring relationship. Ruth, a graduate student and research fellow in her mid-fifties, met Lorraine serendipitously at a coffee bar. They soon discovered shared interests and professional connections. As Ruth talked, Lorraine, a stay-at-home mother with a master's degree, was suddenly transported back into a world she had not realized she missed. Ruth sensed Lorraine's interest and invited her to attend a seminar she was conducting at a nearby university. Just two days later, Lorraine was back in a graduate school classroom—fascinated, mesmerized, and totally immersed.

A month later, Ruth recruited Lorraine to join a project team doing part-time research. Lorraine was not sure she was ready for the challenge, but with Ruth's support, Lorraine exceeded even her own expectations, which she attributed to Ruth, who had become her mentor.

Ruth listened as Lorraine shared her new experiences and provided regular feedback (*managing the process*). She coached Lorraine about how to use a variety of research tools and methodologies and provided support (*maintaining momentum*). When Lorraine had moments of doubt about how to apply her new knowledge, Ruth encouraged her to experiment with what she was learning (*encouraging movement*). After several years, Lorraine become project team leader.

Ruth facilitated Lorraine's learning by managing the learning process and providing appropriate support, maintaining the momentum as Lorraine faced challenges, and encouraging movement, which enabled growth and continuous learning. Ruth's adeptness at providing continuous feedback effectively accelerated the learning curve.

Support, challenge, and vision help the mentor nurture mentee growth throughout a mentoring relationship, and particularly during the enabling phase. Of the three, support is the most critical because it lays the foundation for challenge and vision.

Support

Mentors manage the mentoring process by providing a safety net, holding a place for connection, and offering a wellspring of trust (Daloz, 1999). One mentee who made a career transition during the midpoint of his career underscored the importance of his mentor's support: "Since the start of our mentor-mentee relationship, Ed has always made time to discuss my career aspirations and has been very supportive during my times of uncertainty. His guidance has had a significant influence over my approach to learn the business outside of the financial field."

The key tasks in providing support are creating a learning environment and building and maintaining the relationship. When mentors listen, provide structure, express positive expectations, serve as advocates, share themselves, and make the relationship special (Daloz, 1999), mentees are most likely to feel supported.

Creating a Learning Environment

Learning environment describes the dynamic climate in which learning takes place. It encompasses a varying combination of elements that can include the behavior and attitude of both mentor and mentee, the physical setting, resources, and opportunity. Mentor support is a critical force in creating a learning environment that facilitates mentee growth and development.

Mentors must look for multiple opportunities to support mentee learning. The questions in Exercise 6.1 can be helpful in thinking about possible learning opportunities. Once you have generated these, you may want to solicit input from others. For example, if the learning goal articulated during the negotiating phase was to prepare the mentee to assume a new position, you might consult with others who are in similar positions to find out what kinds of opportunities helped them or would have helped prepare them for a new role.

The list in Exercise 6.2 is provided as a resource to assist in identifying opportunities for learning to supplement the list you developed in completing Exercise 6.1. You may choose to complete the exercise with your mentee.

The learning that takes place in connection with a particular opportunity is often just as important as the opportunity itself. Let us say that Gary, Georgina, and Harry (all mentees) are going to attend an off-site team meeting with Myrna, their mentor. Prior to attending the meeting, Myrna prepares them for what they will see and likely experience. She describes the

EXERCISE 6.1

Generating a List of Learning Opportunities

Instructions: Use this chart to record ideas that come to mind as you think about the topic "possible learning opportunities." Ask yourself:

- What opportunities are available in-house?

- What is available outside the office?

- What kinds of opportunities exist to get exposure to new learning?

- What kinds of opportunities exist to reinforce new learning?

- What kinds of opportunities exist that might accelerate learning?

Possible Learning Opportunities Where?		Possible Learning Opportunities What for?		
In-house	Outside the office	To gain exposure to new learning	To reinforce new learning	To accelerate learning

EXERCISE 6.2

Identifying Learning Opportunities

Instructions: For each category, list specific learning opportunities that fit with your mentee's learning goals.

Opportunities to get exposure to new learning

- Conferences

- Trade shows

- Meetings

- Books, articles

-

-

Opportunities to reinforce new learning

- Committee and project assignments

- Attending office meetings together

- Check-in conversations (telephone or e-mail)

- Planning an event together

-

-

Opportunities to accelerate learning

- Stretch assignments

- Shadowing (observing the mentor or another individual in action)

-

-

purpose of the meeting, who will be attending, the role of each of the participants, and identifies specific things for them to look for during the meeting. As soon as possible after the meeting, Myrna meets with Gary, Georgina, and Harry to process the meeting, identify what has been learned, and reconnect their outcomes to their learning goals.

Building and Maintaining the Relationship

Creating a supportive learning climate ultimately rests on building and maintaining relationships. Without building and maintaining a learning relationship, effective mentoring is impossible. Building and maintaining a mentoring relationship involves respect, trust, and effective communication.

Respect

Some mentors put considerable stock in personal chemistry, as if it were the "be all and end all" of a mentoring relationship. Mentees and mentors look to affinity, camaraderie, harmony, bonding, and similarity as the litmus test for mentoring chemistry. If the litmus paper fails to turn color, some mentoring partners simply write off the relationship, missing an opportunity for learning. It is possible to mentor successfully even if the chemistry does not feel quite right. Respect, not chemistry, helps individuals to engage effectively and learn from one another. Sometimes mentoring partners take respect for granted and, as a result, fail to build rapport and earn each other's trust.

Trust

Sometimes people equate respect with trust. The truth of the matter is that you can respect another person yet not trust him or her. Both respect and trust are important in a mentoring relationship.

Trust needs to be built over time. In order to build trust, you will need to do the following:

- Listen in ways that show you respect your mentee and that you value his or her ideas.

- Practice openness when sharing information.

- Speak authentically about your feelings.

- Explain what you understand and admit when you do not understand something.

- Explain why you shift the level of your support according to the situation.

- Follow through. Do what you say you will do.

- Continuously work at safeguarding confidentiality.

- Be open to feedback.
- Be truthful.
- Be consistent.
- Be supportive publicly and privately.

Because mentoring partners have built trust does not mean that it will be maintained. Mentoring partners have to build trust continuously. Without it, there is little authenticity in the relationship. Trust is directly linked to effective communication.

Communication

The potential for mistrust and miscommunication in a mentoring relationship should not be taken lightly. That is precisely the reason that establishing and honoring ground rules for communication is so important. Ground rules are like a safety valve for the relationship. Once they are articulated, both partners have a common set of understandings about their communication to which they can refer.

Mentors and mentees with different styles often develop misunderstandings and conflict more as a result of style than substantive differences. Therefore, it is important to be aware of your own and your mentee's communication style. The knowledge will help shape your communication and your responses accordingly.

Some might describe Chad as personable, friendly, energetic, and enthusiastic. He loves to be with people. His mentee, Nate, appears reserved and shy. Chad uses broad brush strokes to paint the big picture, while Nate is practical, orderly, and realistic. Chad is a quick decision maker, while it takes Nate time to process information. In style, the two could not be diametrically more opposed. However, having had an opportunity to talk about their opposite styles, Chad became aware that he could not impose his style on Nate and would need to be more specific in his interaction. Nate realized that he would need to be more open and outgoing in order to get his needs met. Together they set up some ground rules that allowed them to talk openly without misconstruing style for conflict.

Challenge

The learning goals of the mentoring relationship set a creative tension in motion that seeks its resolution through execution of the mentoring agreement. As mentors challenge mentees to close the learning gap, they help them move from present reality to future action. They maintain that momentum by setting tasks, engaging in discussion, setting up dichotomies, constructing hypotheses, and setting high standards (Daloz, 1999). Monitoring the learning process and evaluating progress toward achievement of learning goals are the mentor's key tasks. They keep the relationship focused on achievement of the learning goals.

Monitoring the Process

There is much to be learned from the mentoring process that can strengthen the relationship. When mentoring partners regularly discuss their mentoring relationship, the conversation helps to maintain the momentum of the relationship and contributes value to the learning of each mentoring partner.

Monitoring does not need to be a cumbersome process, but it should be regular, whether it is once a month or every quarter. Exercise 6.3 can be used to focus conversation about meetings, relationships, and learning. Although the worksheet can be used in several ways, it is particularly helpful when each partner completes it independently and then both partners discuss their results. It lends itself equally well to cybermentoring or face-to-face mentoring. As a result of regular mentoring partnership reflection, communication is improved, partners can make midcourse corrections, and mentoring pitfalls can be circumvented. Completed discussion guides can be used as a stimulus for conversation following the next mentoring partnership reflection.

Mentoring Interaction

It is helpful for mentors (and mentees) to monitor the quality of the mentoring interaction. It also affords an opportunity to do some reflection on the relationship in preparation for a forthcoming mentoring conversation. Exercise 6.4 provides a form to use to accomplish that purpose.

One mentor who had been meeting with a mentee for several years completed this exercise and realized that the quality of interaction in her mentoring relationship was no longer satisfactory. Although she knew that on a visceral level, she had never actually articulated it to herself. The act of disciplining herself to reflect and analyze the situation forced her to realize that she needed to pump new life into the relationship or end it. She began to think about what she had contributed to the current situation and decided that her desire to meet at 6:00 A.M. each Tuesday was not productive. Neither was the small talk that diverted their conversation from the real purpose of the relationship. Reflection forced a conversation that she

EXERCISE 6.3

Mentoring Partnership Reflection: A Discussion Guide

Instructions: There are three ways to use this form: (1) Each mentoring partner completes this form independently and then discusses individual responses. (2) Mentoring partners discuss each item and complete the form together. (3) Each time a mentoring partnership reflection is completed, it is saved and used as a starting point for conversation or as a follow up to (1) above.

Meetings

1. When and under what circumstances did we get together?

2. Generally when we got together, what did we talk about? (List subjects or topics.)

3. What objectives are we working on right now? What is our progress to date in achieving these objectives?

Relationship

1. What is going particularly well in our mentoring relationship right now?

2. What has been our greatest challenge in our mentoring partnership so far?

3. What do we need to work at to improve our mentoring relationship?

4. What assistance could we use?

Learning

1. What are we learning about ourselves? Each other? The relationship?

2. What is being learned? What are some of the conditions that promote that learning?

3. What are some of the personal insights? Hunches? Things to watch for?

EXERCISE 6.4

Monitoring the Quality of the Mentoring Interaction

Instructions: Answer the following questions to monitor the quality of the mentoring interaction and to prepare for the following mentoring session. You may want to encourage your mentee to fill out a version of this as well and then use it as a basis for discussion. When entries are collated, the tool can become a useful developmental log for evaluating progress with respect to interaction in the relationship.

1. What are some of the words or phrases you would use to describe the current interaction?

2. Describe your interaction.

3. Assess where your mentee is on the continuum from dependent to interdependent learner.

|---------------------------|---------------------------|---------------------------|

Dependent   Independent   Interdependent

4. To what extent would you describe the interaction as authentic and genuine?

5. Are the frequency and duration of interaction adequate? If not, what needs to be done to correct the situation?

6. How would my mentee characterize her relationship with me?

7. What action strategies do I need to take to improve the quality of the mentoring interaction? My personal contribution?

might not otherwise have had. She and her mentee were able to talk about how the relationship was going and what each could do to strengthen it. They also realized in the process that they had accomplished more than either of them had thought. The problem was that they had failed to communicate that reality to each other.

Regular Check-In

Even if the relationship seems to be going well, checking on its health helps to ensure that the needs of the mentoring partners are being met. Exercise 6.5 presents a framework for monitoring the learning process on a regular basis.

Evaluating Progress

Mentee goals are the cornerstone of the mentoring relationship. As the benchmarks for measuring progress, they should therefore be referred to frequently. The objectives outlined on the mentoring planning form (Exercise 5.5) and the goal statement articulated in the mentoring partnership agreement become personal benchmarks for evaluating progress toward achievement of learning goals. Evaluating progress regularly helps maintain momentum, keeps learning goals at the forefront of the relationship, and holds partners accountable for achieving the goals.

The mentoring planning form thus becomes the measuring stick from which to measure progress. If you make copies and have it available at each

EXERCISE 6.5

Checking In: A Framework for Conversation

Instructions: Use any of the following conversation starters to provide a framework for beginning discussion about the learning process.

1. Check in at the beginning of your meeting. Regularly ask the question, "How is it going?"

2. Share your observations about how things are going and what concerns you have about the learning process—for example, "I've noticed that our discussions are very general and theoretical. Are you finding them helpful?"

3. Take a step backward before you go forward—for example, "Let's take a look at how we are doing. What is particularly helpful to you in your learning? What has been least helpful? What do you think is going well? What do we need to improve? What kind of assistance do you need?"

mentoring session, you can refer to it. It can be used in conjunction with Exercise 6.5 (expanding the question you use so it includes reference to learning goals) to frame a conversation on evaluation of progress.

Mentoring partners should be aware of where they are at any given moment relative to meeting learning goals. Regularly measuring progress is an accountability tool for the partnership. It also helps identify possible obstacles.

Vision

Because of their experience and the vision they hold up, mentors can guide a mentee's sense of the possible. The mentor's vision inspires and informs. Sharing stories, modeling behavior, and holding up a mirror empower the mentee. By fostering continuous reflection and assessing learning outcomes, movement is encouraged during and after completion of the relationship.

Fostering Reflection

Reflection, a process for enabling mentees to take the long view by stepping back and then moving forward, helps create a vision of what might be. "Through reflection we bring our actions to consciousness, reinterpret situations in light of the consequences of our behavior, identify performance gaps, and conceptualize ways for improving our practice in the future" (Lewis and Dowling, 1992).

Reflective practice emerges from experience. By asking the right questions at the right time, mentors stimulate mentees to reflect on their experiences and frame their interpretations into suitable actions (Rose, 1992). Thus, experiences become the text for learning, and the do-reflect-learn-act cycle—Schön's (1983) reflection-in-action model—is set in motion as the springboard for learning.

Mentors must model reflection-in-action. The exercises presented in this book are intended to foster reflective mentoring practice and thus generate new insights for mentor and mentee.

Assessing Learning Outcomes

When ongoing monitoring and evaluation are part of the mentoring relationship routine, assessing learning outcomes becomes a natural outgrowth of those conversations.

Assessing outcomes may be appropriate when a particular learning objective or cluster of objectives has been completed. It is especially important in deciding when the time has come to end a mentoring relationship. It helps prepare the mentee for the transition out of the relationship and helps to create the vision for the future that follows closure of the relationship. It also places accountability squarely back on the shoulders of the mentee.

The assessment of learning outcomes conversation is more than a "check-in" conversation. This conversation can have the benefit of feedback from a variety of sources. The mentee may choose to seek objective feedback from coworkers, colleagues, family, and friends, in addition to subjective evaluation with the mentoring partner.

The point is that assessing learning outcomes relates to the mentee's specific learning objectives. It is not a matter of checking items off a list, but of getting accurate feedback that forces continuous improvement and ongoing learning.

Strategic Enabling Processes

Two strategic enabling processes permeate support, challenge, and vision: engaging in meaningful feedback and overcoming obstacles.

Engaging in Meaningful Feedback

Feedback is a powerful vehicle for learning and a critical enabling mechanism in facilitating mentoring relationships. It is impossible to create a learning environment, build and maintain the relationship, monitor process, evaluate progress, foster reflection, and assess learning outcomes without it. When feedback is given and received in the right way, it nurtures the growth of the mentoring relationship. When it is given or received in the wrong way, it can undermine the relationship. Being able to ask for feedback, receive it, accept it, and take action because of it can spell the difference between success and failure in a mentoring relationship.

The mentor's challenge is to provide thoughtful, candid, and constructive feedback in a manner that supports individual learning and development while encouraging the mentee's authorship and expression in meeting new challenges.

Enriching the Feedback Process

Mentors enrich the feedback process when they take the time to develop a climate of readiness and expectation. Providing feedback without establishing a climate of readiness can be a frustrating and negative experience for mentees and mentors.

The following general guidelines are useful for mentors in providing feedback in a mentoring relationship:

- Build rapport.

- Set clear expectations about the feedback you provide, acknowledging the limits of that feedback.

- Be authentic and candid.

- Focus on behaviors, not personality.

- Provide feedback regularly.

- Ask for feedback on your feedback. Make sure that the feedback you are providing is meeting the specific needs of your mentee. Ask: Was this feedback helpful? In what ways?

- Consider the timing of the feedback.

- Make constructive comments.

The feedback circle illustrated in Exhibit 6.2 extends the linear "asking for–receiving model" of feedback into a more expansive cyclical approach: asking for feedback, giving feedback, receiving feedback, accepting feedback, and acting on feedback.

EXHIBIT 6.2

The Feedback Circle

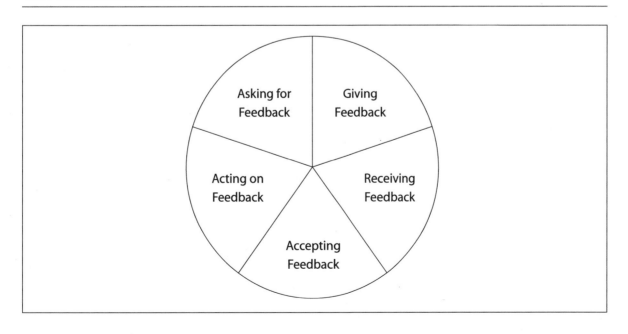

Asking for Feedback Because they are self-directed, learners who invite feedback are able to accomplish more than those who are not. Sometimes, however, a mentee is unfamiliar with the feedback process and does not know how to ask for feedback or is uncomfortable asking for it. Lack of experience, lack of power, feeling intimidated or inadequate, and fear of revealing personal vulnerabilities are typical hurdles that mentees identify as getting in the way of asking for feedback. Mentors who encourage mentees to take initiative in asking for feedback encourage self-direction.

Roger is studying for the clergy and has been paired with a mentor who holds a senior clergy position in a large urban congregation. His mentor, Marcus, is easygoing and a great conversationalist who is always open to questions. Roger knows that he is lucky to have Marcus as a mentor but feels that his mentor is leaving too much to him in the relationship. Roger feels that Marcus never initiates, directs, or guides him and lets him talk about whatever he wants to doing their sessions. Roger feels he is not getting the support he needs because he does not know enough to ask the right questions.

Sometimes mentors need to coach mentees, like Roger, in how to ask for feedback, what to expect from feedback, and the importance of feedback in the mentoring relationship. When and if this happens, it is helpful to find out what the mentee's experience has been with asking for feedback and what, if any, hesitation he or she might have. The list of talking points in Exercise 6.6 can shape the conversation about how to assist the mentee to ask for feedback.

EXERCISE 6.6
Guidelines for Asking for Feedback

Instructions: Review the following items before framing an initial discussion about feedback with a mentee. They can also be used following a feedback interaction as checkpoints for review.

- Be specific and descriptive in asking for feedback.
- Make sure that what you are asking for is clear and understandable.
- Stay focused.
- Avoid being defensive.
- Seek alternatives, not answers.
- Check for understanding.
- Make sure you are getting what you need.
- Ask for feedback on a regular basis.

Giving Feedback Giving feedback may be one of the most valuable and challenging aspects of the mentor's role. Daloz (1999, p. 212) cautions that "balancing the imperative of providing 'honest feedback' with the equally compelling need to let them [learners] know that they 'can do it' is enough to strain the best of us."

Three factors are potential barriers to providing effective feedback to a mentee: mentor attitude and comfort level, feedback requests, and organizational situations.

Mentor attitude and comfort level. Mentors who are hesitant to provide the feedback being requested should reflect on three questions: How comfortable am I with providing feedback? (Refer to Exercise 4.4, Mentoring Skills Inventory.) Is my personal reaction to getting feedback affecting my attitude? How can I best provide the information in ways that promote learning?

Request for feedback. Before responding to a request for specific feedback, the mentor should be able to answer each of the following questions in the affirmative:

- Is the request for feedback clear?

- Do I have adequate information in order to understand the reason for the request?

- Is the request or inquiry an appropriate or reasonable one?

- Is there enough time to respond to the request adequately?

- Is what is being asked really what the person is asking?

Consideration of these questions can assist in identifying possible barriers before providing feedback.

Specific organizational situations. It may be that particular practices and procedures in a mentee's organization discourage candid feedback. For example, some organizational cultures make an effort to avoid conflict. As a result, honest feelings are submerged.

In some situations and under some circumstances, it may not be appropriate to give feedback. A mentor who suspects that this is the case should consider the following questions

- Am I the right person in this organization to provide this feedback?

- Am I compromising another person's role by giving feedback?

- Is this the right time in this person's career (and/or in this organization or institution) to provide the feedback being requested?

- What opportunities are available within the organization that will allow the mentee to apply this knowledge?

- How would others within the organization react to the advice I have given?

- Is the feedback going to be consistent with the policies of the organization and aligned with the organization's mission?

The mentor's goal in providing feedback is to facilitate learning. Learning cannot be facilitated unless the feedback is relevant, practical, and specific. Giving feedback is not as simple as offering advice or constructive criticism. It is an act of care that requires knowing what to do and how to give it meaningfully. Exhibit 6.3 offers some practical tips and examples.

Receiving Feedback Throughout the enabling phase, mentees and mentors receive feedback. The mentor should be receiving feedback throughout the relationship on the process and the content of the learning. The mentee receives feedback throughout the learning relationship. Receiving feedback is not a passive activity. It is an open, interactive, clarifying, and confirming conversation.

One mentor, engaged in a long-distance mentoring relationship, concluded an e-mail note to his mentee, an aspiring writer, by saying, "Anyway, I hope this is somewhat helpful. Let's stay in touch with all this. Let me know what is helpful and what is not. We'll stay on this." With these four short sentences, he invited feedback, left the door open for further conversation, and stated a desire to be helpful and supportive. The mentee who received this comment, along with written feedback, felt validated. Her mentor had reinforced the fact that it would be the mentee's responsibility to continue the conversation.

When receiving feedback, mentoring partners need to keep an open mind so that what is being said is heard. Remaining open to the experience avoids the creation of a situation where the mentor or mentee is fighting negative feedback. One way to make sure that feedback has been heard as it was intended is to encourage the mentee to summarize understandings and feelings when feedback is received. Taking this time provides an opportunity for further clarification.

Andrew, a middle school language teacher, was experiencing difficulty in managing the students in his classroom. With each passing day, the challenge of rambunctious seventh and eighth graders was becoming more than he could handle. He tried being more directive, showing his displeasure, and even setting up some classroom ground rules, but nothing seemed to be working. Andrew shared his concerns with his mentor. His mentor listened for a while and then encouraged him to describe the behaviors of the students that were troubling to him and his response to those behaviors. As his mentor offered suggestions and options for action, he encouraged Andrew to respond, ask questions, and check for understanding. The experience of

EXHIBIT 6.3

Tips for Mentors in Providing Feedback

What to Do	How to Do It	Example
Align your feedback with the mentee's agenda.	Provide real-time feedback. Make it usable and realistic. Offer concrete practical steps and options.	"I have a few ideas that might help …" "What works for me is …"
Provide feedback about behavior that the mentee can do something about.	Stay with the mentee's behavior rather than succumb to the temptation to evaluate it.	"Tell me about the impact of the behavior …" "How might someone else see that behavior?"
When you talk from your perspective, remember that your reality is not the mentee's reality.	When you talk about your own experience, set a context and be descriptive so that the mentee can see the parallels.	"In my experience, which was …, I found that … I know that is not your situation, but maybe there is something to learn here."
Check out your understanding of what is being said.	Listen actively. Clarify and summarize.	"If I understand what you are saying …" "Help me understand what you mean by …"
Use a tone of respect.	Take care not to undermine the mentee's self-esteem.	"I liked the way you …" "I am curious …" "I wonder …" "Have you ever considered …?"
Be aware of your communication style and how that works with that of your mentee.	Share information about communication styles with your mentee, and discuss the implications for the feedback cycle.	"I find that I get defensive when …" "I react positively to …"
Avoid giving feedback when you lack adequate information.	Ask for time to get the information you need. Faking it doesn't work.	"To be honest with you, I need to think about that a little more."
Encourage the mentee to experience feedback as movement forward rather than interruption from the journey.	Continuously link progress and learning to the big picture and the journey.	"When we started out … And then … And now …"

checking for understanding provided new insights for Andrew and also suggested to him that perhaps he needed to check for understanding with his students.

Accepting Feedback Strong reactions to feedback are natural. Sometimes the recipient of the feedback reacts with denial or resistance. The feedback recipient needs to get past the reactive or resistive mode in order to integrate new learning. A mentee in denial about the feedback may appear to be surprised, even shocked, perhaps stating outright, "That's not my problem!" In this situation, the mentor should present information linking the past to the present and future outcomes and then present a strategy or suggestion that demonstrates the benefits of the particular strategy (the answer to the question, "What's in it for me?").

If a mentee appears to be resisting feedback, it could be that the mentee doubts his or her ability, feels hurt, or blames others for the current situation. A mentor who lets the mentee who is resisting feedback vent before offering suggestions is being supportive. Sometimes the venting can be done during the interaction; at other times, space and time are needed.

Some individuals appear to have boundless energy once they receive feedback. Mentors can be helpful by focusing the mentee on priority setting so that he or she can identify a new course of action and consider new possibilities.

Acting on Feedback Action, not reaction, is the ultimate goal of feedback. Here is where a mentor must encourage a mentee to move forward to meet new challenges and, as the feedback cycle begins again, be ready to provide feedback, ask challenging questions, and help the mentee integrate new learnings. This is truly an opportunity for reflection-in-action (Schön, 1983). It may be helpful to encourage the mentee to develop a step-by-step action plan (and perhaps a contingency plan) with follow-up and accountability mechanisms and ask for feedback on that plan.

The Gift of Feedback

There is no greater contribution to mentee learning than the gift a mentor provides by giving and receiving ongoing, honest, constructive feedback. Expanding the capacity of a mentee to do the same promotes competence, inspires confidence, and enriches the learning experience. When mentoring partners are prepared to engage in a meaningful feedback process, overcoming obstacles is made easier.

Overcoming Obstacles

Overcoming obstacles is the second of the two strategic enabling processes embedded in the three conditions that facilitate learning. Every relationship faces obstacles at one time or another. The challenge is to overcome them and learn from the experience. A mentor who is familiar with how to support, challenge, and provide vision can facilitate mentee growth and development despite the obstacles that present themselves.

In any relationship there are always lurking dangers—possible obstacles and stumbling blocks—that threaten to affect the dynamics of the relationship. The enabling phase, where mentoring partners spend the bulk of their mentoring time, is fraught with lurking dangers.

Elaine and Darlene's* relationship illustrates many of the lurking dangers that threaten mentoring relationships during the enabling phase. Elaine, forty-three years old, is a concerned, compassionate, and resourceful mentor. Having raised two children alone while working full time and earning a master's degree, she is committed to helping other women do the same.

Darlene, thirty-three years old, is divorced with a twelve-year-old daughter and a six-year-old son. She has a history of family dysfunction: parental abuse, neglect, and alcoholism. When she relocated to a new community to start over, she was offered the opportunity of working with a mentor.

Elaine's motivation to become a mentor was connected to her work as a counselor. Having raised two children as a struggling single mom, she felt she could offer the direction and motivation Darlene need to grow both socially and professionally.

Elaine and Darlene developed rapport instantly, and both looked forward to the new learning that the mentoring relationship would bring them. However, their excitement was short-lived. Soon both experienced dissatisfaction. Elaine reported she was frustrated because, as she reported to the mentoring coordinator, "Darlene seems to have issues of entitlement." All Elaine's efforts to move Darlene toward personal and professional growth were met with comments like these: "I don't think so"; "Yes, but," and, "I tried that already." The few goals Darlene did set were soon discarded.

Elaine remained committed to her drive to help Darlene to reach self-sufficiency and a higher quality of life, remembering her own difficulties as

*I wish to thank Ceah Ure, former mentoring director of the Fresh Start Women's Foundation, Phoenix, Arizona, for developing this example.

a single parent without support. Elaine even researched a scholarship to summer camp for Darlene's son and provided a list of agencies that could assist her in relocating to a better neighborhood with her children. But the longer they worked together, the more Darlene met Elaine's efforts with excuses, resistance, and reasons not to follow through.

As time wore on, Darlene either failed to show up for scheduled appointments or would bring her son, who was often disruptive. Darlene's negativism increased as she insisted she was simply "a victim once again" and "not understood." She regularly complained about her mother's negative influence on her, her children's fighting, and the problems in her housing complex. Still, Darlene refused to consider making any change.

After four months, Elaine had had enough. She blurted out, "I feel burned out and used. I worked very hard to get Darlene the free tuition to summer camp for her son. I cannot understand why she turned down the offer. I raised two boys alone. I know how hard it is to be a single mother. If someone offered me the help I offered Darlene, I would have been grateful and accepting. I really do not think she wants to be helped. I don't think I am able to motivate Darlene to make meaningful changes in her life."

Among other things in this situation, we see a mentee who is sabotaging the relationship (not showing up, being disruptive) and passively participating in this relationship (her attitude of entitlement, resistance to help). Elaine was stressed, burned out, and projecting her own needs on her mentee. She has assumed that she was standing in Darlene's shoes but had not ascertained if her assumptions were correct. The relationship suffered from lack of goals, trust, and inauthentic communication. Elaine may have been in denial about where the relationship was headed; Darlene was clearly in resistance. The wall that had built up was too tall for either of them to scale. The relationship did not work because each had contributed to the toxic situation they found themselves in.

Mentors should be aware that lurking dangers are an ever-present dynamic in mentoring relationships. By recognizing the obstacles that mentees can bring to the relationship and obstacles that mentors bring on themselves, mentors and mentees can anticipate problems and preserve productive relationships. Some people, however, just do not belong in a mentoring relationship. When this is the case, mentors need to reset boundaries and limits or bring the relationship to closure.

Strategies for Overcoming Obstacles with Mentees

- Consume-you mentees. The mentees who assume entitlement often have a user mentality and are exploitative of mentor knowledge and time.

Strategy: Avoid becoming your mentee's 411 (for all information) or 911 (emergency road and rescue service). If you let that happen, you become a co-dependent and a possible victim of mentor abuse.

- Jealous mentees. When mentees grow or advance beyond their mentors, resentment often builds up, and they perceive a mentor as holding them back.

  Strategy: This is a signal for closure. Be sure to focus on learning conclusions and appropriate celebration and then move on.

- Peripatetic mentees. Unfocused mentees are all over the place. They ask for advice but show little follow-through or commitment.

  Strategy: At each mentoring session, focus on the goals of the relationship and preplanned agenda. At the end of the session, review how much progress there has been against the goals and agenda.

- Manipulative mentees. These mentees forever seek favors, opportunities, and control in the relationship. Mentors in this situation can feel used and resentful.

  Strategy: This is the time to revisit boundaries and roles in the mentoring partnership agreement.

- Apathetic mentees. Some mentees lack candor, good intention, and follow-through. They are not prepared or committed to the relationship and seek just to get their immediate needs met.

  Strategy: A mentee who lacks internal motivation sees little reason to follow through. The goal is to get commitment by clarifying goals and roles. Perhaps the mentee does not have a clear understanding of roles and responsibilities. Or there may be a lack of commitment to goals because they are not specific and clear enough.

Strategies for Mentors to Overcome Their Own Obstacles

- Impostership. This notion, first introduced by Brookfield (1995), has to do with the expectation that a mentor needs to be all things to a mentee.

  Strategy: Mentors who do not manage their self-expectations set themselves up for failure. Be clear about what you do not know. Do not expect to be able to do it all or provide it all.

- Burnout. Mentors who take on too much in the relationship or let themselves be manipulated may burn out.

  Strategy: When mentoring becomes a burden, try to figure out why and then do something about it.

- Stress. Mentoring is one of many other commitments and situations in life going on at the same time. And there are always situations beyond a mentor's control.

  Strategy: Call time-out if you need to lessen stress. Mentoring should not be stressful.

- Lack of disclosure. Being unwilling to share information and feelings may create a situation where mentees read more into communication than is intended.

  Strategy: Be straightforward, firm, and up front in your communication.

- Ethical dilemmas. Mentors sometimes get pushed where they do not want to go. In the desire to meet a mentee's learning needs, mentors may find themselves in a situation where they need to make ethical decisions.

  Strategy: Be on the alert, and stay true to yourself.

- Crossing boundaries. Mentors need to let mentees know when a boundary has been crossed.

  Strategy: Don't make it personal. Use the mentoring partnership agreement as a point of reference, and begin the conversation there.

- Prejudice and bias. Prejudice of any kind (gender, racial, ethnic) has no place in a mentoring relationship.

  Strategy: If you find that you are exhibiting prejudice or your biases are getting in the way, it is time to consider closure.

- Procrastination. When mentors find themselves rescheduling mentoring meetings or putting off mentoring conversations, it is time to consider why this is happening.

  Strategy: It may be a time crunch issue or a signal for closure.

- Jealousy. Mentors may experience jealousy if a mentee advances beyond them.

  Strategy: Express pride in your mentee's accomplishments. Then decide if it is time for you to move on. If that is the situation, help the mentee set new goals or find a new mentor.

- *Chain of command.* When the mentor also signs the paycheck, the intimidation factor comes into play.

  Strategy: Mentors can have a productive mentoring relationship with someone in their chain of command if they are clear about the boundaries of the relationship. Keep lines of communication open, and focus on the learner's questions and needs.

During the enabling stage, it is particularly important to acknowledge lurking dangers as they occur. Purposeful discussion can dispel tension by bringing things out in the open that might later become undiscussable. An example might be breach of confidence. Addressing the situation results in reevaluation or renegotiation rather than abortive termination.

A Recap

The list of ways to support mentees in the enabling phase is long, mirroring the duration of the phase (see Exhibit 6.4). This phase is really the process phase, and accordingly, there is no beginning, middle, and end to the process tasks in it. These processes continue throughout the duration of the relationship. The signal to move on is when the learning goals have been accomplished.

Moving Through

It is easy to see why the enabling phase is so challenging. Its unexpected delights, vast opportunities, learning challenges, and lurking dangers present relationship peaks and valleys.

EXHIBIT 6.4

How to Support the Mentee in the Enabling Phase

- From time to time, reread the job descriptions of all parties involved in this relationship.
- Establish a regular pattern of contact.
- Meet on a regular basis.
- Continuously monitor the relationship to make sure that the relationships are objective driven.
- Expect to make midcourse corrections.
- Expect the relationship to take time to develop.
- Periodically ask yourself, "What am I learning?"
- Remember that the mentor's role is to provide professional guidance to the mentee. Keep behavior consistent with the parameters of such a relationship.
- Be on the constant lookout for learning opportunities.
- Consider multiple options for connection.
- Give the relationship space.
- Provide regular feedback to your mentoring partner.
- Be consistent in your participation.

EXERCISE 6.7

Enabling Questions: A Readiness Checklist

Instructions: Answer each of the questions below, adding examples after each response.

- Am I providing adequate support to facilitate the learning of my mentee?

- Have we identified sufficient and varied opportunities and venues for learning?

- Are we continuing to build and maintain a productive relationship?

- Is the quality of our mentoring interaction satisfactory?

- Are we continuously working on improving the quality of the mentoring interaction?

- Are we continuing to work at maintaining the trust in this relationship?

- Have we put in place a variety of mechanisms to ensure continuous feedback?

- Is the feedback I am giving thoughtful, candid, and constructive?

- Do we make time to reflect on our partnership regularly?

- Are there lurking dangers or subjects too difficult to discuss in the mentoring relationship?

The readiness checklist for the enabling phase differs from those presented in previous chapters. Readiness in this case is about moving through rather than moving on. With that in mind, you may find it helpful to come back to Exercise 6.7 periodically to make sure that you stay on track. From time to time, you may find that you answer some of the items negatively. When that is the case, the checklist is useful as an indicator that you need to work on strengthening the support, challenge, and vision you are providing.

You will know you are ready to move on to closure when the mentee's learning goals have been completed.

CHAPTER 7

Reaping the Harvest

Coming to Closure

For every gardener knows that after the digging, after the planting,
after the long season of tending and growth, the harvest comes.
—MARGE PIERCY, "The Seven of Pentacles"

Coming to closure presents the greatest challenge for mentoring partners, for many reasons. Ending a relationship is often beset with anxiety, resentment, or surprise. It is difficult to plan for closure because relationships can end earlier or last longer than anticipated. Sometimes partners hang on indefinitely, neither of them wanting to let go because of the emotions and personal ties inherent in the relationship. Sometimes inertia or a sense of comfort sustains a mentoring relationship long after it should otherwise end. In a planned mentoring program, a specific end date of the program cycle usually dictates when the relationship should end. The result is that partners sometimes stay in mentoring relationships even though the learning goals have been achieved, or they conclude on time but without having achieved learning goals.

Coming to closure is an evolving process. The seeds for closure are planted in the negotiating phase, when the mentoring partners establish closure protocols and develop a mentoring partnership agreement. The process itself begins the moment that mentoring partners start working toward accomplishment of learning goals.

This seemingly short phase offers opportunity for growth and reflection regardless of whether the relationship has been positive. Coming to closure presents a developmental opportunity for mentors and mentees to harvest their learning and move on. If closure is to be a mutually satisfying learning experience, mentoring partners must be prepared for it.

This chapter advocates intentional inclusion of closure protocols and processes as a requisite part of mentoring. Emphasis is placed on the need to plan for closure in ways that both acknowledge and recognize the time for closure and ensure that closure is a satisfying and meaningful learning experience for mentoring partners.

The Case for Closure

Closure always has an emotional component: discomfort, anxiety, fear, disappointment, relief, grief, fear of separation, joy, or excitement. Acknowledging these emotions and moving on is an expected part of the separation process. Dealing with them takes more time than most people anticipate.

In general, individuals who have difficulty ending relationships will experience the most difficulty dealing with closure in a mentoring relationship. For them, the hardest part is letting go. It is particularly problematic when neither partner knows how to or lacks positive experience in ending relationships. Similarly, when mentoring partners become friends and drift into a more informal relationship based on the growing familiarity, it is particularly difficult to let go of the mentoring component to the relationship. In such a situation, it is important to mark the transition out of the mentoring relationship and into friendship and use it as an opportunity for learning.

Avoiding Closure

Sometimes mentoring partners prefer to avoid closure because of a fear of hurt feelings or anxiety.

Helen felt obligated to Betsy (her mentor for three years) and was afraid to rock the boat. Although she was not satisfied with their mentoring relationship, Helen did not want to hurt Betsy's feelings, so closure was not an option for her. Helen preferred to let her mentoring relationship run its course and live with the discomfort of obligatory niceness. As a result, she was stuck and unable to move on.

Greg never really felt connected to his mentee, Art. He agreed to be part of the staff mentoring program because it made him look good to have a mentee. As time went on, maintaining the relationship became a chore. Greg too waited and waded through the pretense.

Things were not going well in Helen or Greg's mentoring relationships. In both relationships, no one wanted to take action. No one was comfortable discussing closure, although each knew that the relationship had already ended. If they had held a negotiating conversation early in their relationship, they would have had a preestablished process in place to bring the relationship to closure comfortably.

Unanticipated Ending Without Closure

In many personal mentoring relationships, the priority level of the mentoring relationship shifts for one of the partners and changes the balance of the relationship.

One day Gretchen, a low-level executive in a Fortune 500 company, received a telephone call from her mentor, Sam, telling her that he was being promoted to another division of the company—a promotion that meant immediate relocation to another city. Sam assured Gretchen that he would be in touch "when everything settled down." Gretchen waited two months for Sam to call and then finally called Sam herself and left a message. He never called her back.

It was life circumstances that caused Mark to pull back from everything but the basics at work. His spouse developed a life-threatening illness, and it was all he could do to take care of her and do his job. Ken, his mentee, was disappointed in Mark, but chose not to push and let Mark off the hook by finding another mentor.

In these examples, both Gretchen and Ken had previously articulated their learning goals with their mentors, but the unanticipated closure caught them off guard. The lack of formal closure for Gretchen and Mark foreclosed an opportunity to process what had been accomplished and learned and to celebrate their mentoring relationship.

Caren and Juanita accomplished their learning objectives. They had not discussed closure and drifted from mentoring partnership to friendship without celebrating their own good work together. The common occurrence of change in the nature of the relationship, from mentor to friend, is seductive because it happens imperceptibly. With the new relationship, attention to accountability may wane, and closure with respect to learning goals may appear to be superfluous since the relationship is continuing through friendship.

In all these examples, these partners lacked a preestablished agreement to discuss how to address coming to closure. If each of these mentoring partners had planned this phase, they could have preempted some of the emotional after-effects of not coming to closure and instead would have maximized the positive learning outcomes of the relationship.

Missed Opportunities

The transition to the next stage of the relationship (postrelationship or reengagement) is often attenuated and awkward without closure. Because there is a particular point when the relationship is ready for closure, timing is a critical element. Drawing out the separation process serves neither the mentor nor mentee well and can turn a positive mentoring experience into a negative one.

Closure is also a demarcation between what is (the mentoring relationship) and what will be (perhaps friend, manager, or colleague). Closure helps prevent situations where a mentee might continue to expect access and advice when it is no longer appropriate.

As long as one of the mentoring partners continues to view the relationship as a learning opportunity, ending that relationship can be a valuable source for learning. If there is no other choice but to terminate the relationship, it may be better to make a clean break and discuss what went right and what went wrong. In both scenarios, the mentor and mentee can learn something from the experience.

Even when mentoring partners discuss the inevitability of closure or establish a no-fault learning conclusion agreement early on in the negotiating phase of their relationship, most rarely revisit that agreement when closure is at hand.

Unanticipated Ending with Closure

Most healthy mentoring relationships do not go on indefinitely. At some point, they end. Closure that is planned for is often easier to deal with, but still presents its own set of challenges.

Unanticipated endings occur even in the healthiest mentoring relationships. Whether it is an external event that forces a change in the mentoring relationship or an internal one (due to personal circumstances), planning how to deal with unanticipated obstacles helps mentoring partners know what to do when changing circumstances occur.

Tricia, Marie, and Tom (all mentees) had been mentoring partners with Liam (their mentor) for nearly eight months. Liam had just been pulled into a new project that was going to require increasing amounts of his time over the next six months. Rather than put off telling his mentoring partners about the change in his work responsibilities, Liam confronted the issue head on. He scheduled a meeting at which he told his mentees that he did not know how his new circumstances were going to affect their relationship, but he knew that it would. Together Tricia, Marie, Tom, and Liam agreed that during this change, they would need to be in touch with Liam more sporadically and for shorter periods of time. They also agreed to set up regular on-line get-togethers in the interim. They planned to review the situation in a month's time and if it was not satisfactory to bring the relationship to a formal close.

By squarely facing foreseeable obstacles, these mentoring partners were able to anticipate closure and develop a contingency plan for dealing with closure.

Recognizing the Need for Closure

There are a number of telltale signs and signals that might suggest that it is time to consider coming to closure (see Exhibit 7.1). Mentors who recognize these signals when they first appear should try to validate their perceptions and assumptions. When signals are ignored or overlooked, they can eat away at even a good relationship.

Sometimes there are no overt signals that indicate mentoring partners should come to closure, yet a mentee or mentor may decide to end the relationship. When this happens, it is important for the other person to respect that decision.

Or it may be that a mentee wants to end a mentoring relationship and the mentor does not feel that that decision is a logical or well-reasoned choice. Nevertheless, a wise mentor respects that choice and knows when, and how, to leave the door open in case the mentee's circumstances change. Here are two approaches from mentors who have kept the door open:

"Even though we need to end the formal mentoring relationship now, I want you to know that I am very interested in continuing to know how you are doing and how you are progressing in applying your learning. Please stay in touch, and let me know how you are doing. In fact, how about if we put a date on the calendar now?"

"I know that you are going through a hard time personally right now, and I understand why continuing to meet is no longer feasible. Please let me know when you are ready to pursue your learning goals again. I've enjoyed our relationship, and I'd be glad to work with you again."

EXHIBIT 7.1

Signals That It Might Be Time for Closure

Signals	Possible Indications
When . . .	*It may be that . . .*
I am bored, uninterested, and thinking about other things when I meet with my mentee.	I am just going through the motions, and this relationship is not meaningful or important to me.
My mentee shows up on the scheduled date, and we meet whether or not there is an agenda.	We are meeting just to meet, and there is no real purpose to our meeting.
I begrudge the time I must spend to maintain this relationship. There are other more important and pressing matters I must attend to.	Mentoring is not a high priority for me right now. I am no longer engaged in the relationship.
It feels as if my mentee is hanging on and will not let go.	My mentee has accomplished her learning goals and is ready to move on, but she does not see it that way.
I have run out of things to talk about with my mentee.	We are wasting each other's time.
There has been a consistent breach of confidence.	I do not trust my mentee and need to be selective about what I choose to share.
My mentee listens to my advice or counsel but then does not follow through.	I am spinning my wheels and wasting my time.
We have been meeting for many months and do not seem to be making progress.	Someone else could better fill my mentee's needs.
After most meetings, I feel wrung out, as if my mentee has drained all my energy.	This is not a healthy relationship.
This appears to be a one-way relationship.	I get little, if any, satisfaction from contributing to this mentee's growth.
Being with my mentee is unpleasant and painful.	I do not like or respect my mentee.
My mentee is high maintenance.	My mentee requires a lot more support than I can or want to provide. It may be that I no longer want to continue this relationship.

Planning for Closure

Participation in a mentoring program helps facilitate the process of coming to closure. Mentors in informal mentoring relationships have to be more conscientious about bringing a mentoring relationship to closure because there is no external structure of accountability.

The time to agree on the process for coming to closure is when the mentoring partnership agreement is first negotiated. It is essential to plan the process of coming to closure and consider how it will play out when closure is anticipated as well as when it is not. Using the learning goals of the mentoring relationship as a focal point provides a basis for discussing best-case and worst-case closure scenarios. By identifying potential stumbling blocks, it is easier to plan how to overcome them. To help ensure that the mentoring relationship concludes on a positive note and a learning conclusion results from the mentoring experience, it is helpful to establish a process to acknowledge the need for closure and identify a framework for organizing the learning conclusion conversation.

Frank and Bob's mentoring relationship came to closure when their company's mentoring program cycle ended. They attended the company's formal mentoring luncheon and received certificates acknowledging their participation in the program. Without that formal event, they might not have brought the relationship to closure or acknowledged their accomplishment and mutual appreciation. Knowing that closure was expected triggered a conversation about this phase and provided a rallying point for the transition that was to follow. Because their relationship was part of a formal program, Frank and Bob were able to tailor Bob's learning goals according to the time frame that his company had set. By the time of the final luncheon, Frank and Bob had met these articulated goals and held their closure conversation.

Yvonne and Carlos's informal mentoring relationship resulted in meeting only three of the five learning objectives they had set out to accomplish for the year. When they met to process the learning at the end of the year, they realized that it would be advantageous to continue their mentoring relationship. They talked about what went well for them and what might improve their relationship and then renegotiated a time line for accomplishing the remaining learning goals. Despite the initial time frame they had set, they realized they were not yet ready to end the relationship.

In this case, reaching closure meant renegotiating rather than ending the relationship. It still required engaging in a meaningful closure conversation.

Reaching Closure

An indispensable part of the experience of coming to closure is bringing the relationship to a learning conclusion: a highly focused conversation about specific learning that has taken place during and as a result of the mentoring relationship. It is a blameless, no-fault (Murray, 1991), reflective conversation about both the process and content of the learning.

Jim and his mentee, Carol, had not had a productive mentoring experience. In fact, in just a few short months, they had placed so many demands on one another that they wore themselves out trying to maintain the relationship. By mutual consent (at Jim's instigation), they decided it was time to end the mentoring relationship. They agreed in advance to hold a learning conclusion conversation.

The conversation began with a review of the learning goals. Using that as a personal benchmark, they focused on the specifics of what Carol had learned and what else was needed to reach the remaining learning outcomes. They talked about what went well for them in the relationship and what did not and why. Consequently, Jim realized that he needed to be more focused on mentee needs and that a mentoring relationship required more patience than he had. Carol learned that she needed to take more responsibility for her own learning, to be more focused, and to take risks. The negative aspects of their relationship were softened by focusing the conversation on what each had learned and how they might apply and leverage that knowledge in the future. (Mistakes, failures, and missteps offer rich experience for learning.) Another positive outcome was that Jim identified other mentors with the appropriate expertise and background whom Carol could contact to further her learning. The result was a blameless conversation focused on the learning, with both partners able to take something positive away from the mentoring experience.

Exercise 7.1 offers guidance for shaping a discussion about the learning conclusion conversation. Ideally this conversation will take place as part of the negotiating conversation and will be revisited again toward the end of the enabling phase in preparation for the closure conversation.

Focusing on Mentee Goals

When a mentoring relationship disintegrates or fizzles out, the mentor and mentee have missed an opportunity to reap the harvest of the relationship. Routinely reviewing goals and objectives throughout the relationship keeps the relationship focused on mentee goals and enables mentoring partners

EXERCISE 7.1

Closure Preparation: Steps and Questions

Instructions: Take the steps in column 1 by asking the related questions in column 2.	
Column 1	**Column 2**
Closure Preparation Step	**Question(s)**
1. Revisit your purpose.	What is our goal in working together?
2. Envision a best-case closure.	What would we ideally like to see happen when this mentoring relationship comes to an end? How can we ensure the relationship reaches a learning conclusion?
3. Envision a worst-case closure.	If the ideal is not possible, how can we still ensure a positive learning conclusion? What might get in the way?
4. Plan for mutual accountability.	What will we do to overcome any factors that get in the way of a reaching a learning conclusion?
5. Establish a process for acknowledging the time for closure.	How will we know when it is the right time to bring the relationship to closure?
6. Establish ground rules for the learning conclusion conversation.	What will the agenda be for our learning conclusion conversation?

to take stock of their progress. This process builds momentum and helps to identify the appropriate time for closure.

As soon as goals and objectives have been met, it is time to reflect on what has been learned, celebrate, and move on. When mentoring partners choose to continue the mentoring relationship, it is necessary to articulate new goals, renegotiate the terms of engagement, and review what has worked well in the past and what has gotten in the way.

Integrating What Has Been Learned

Without closure, a mentee can lose the dimension of leveraging the learning that has taken place. Good closure incorporates helping mentoring partners apply and integrate what has been learned as a result of the relationship. A mentor's questions and thoughtful analysis can help a mentee evaluate learning outcomes and identify how to maximize and build on that learning.

For over a year Neal and his mentee, Elliott, have been engaged in a mentoring relationship that came about as a result of a corporate mentoring initiative. In a recent memo from the company's training and development department, Neal was reminded that the year's mentoring cycle was almost through, signaling the need to bring closure to the mentoring relationship.

Neal began the process by sending an e-mail asking Elliott to come to the next mentoring session prepared to review the learning plan they laid out when they started meeting. When they met, Neal focused the conversation on each of the original learning goals and then asked Elliott for his assessment in relation to each of them. Elliott responded that his goal had been to learn how to position himself for new opportunities within the department and that he felt he had made considerable progress. In turn, Neal asked Elliott to describe the progress he felt he had made and to identify how he had specifically applied what he had learned. Once Elliott articulated his response, he and Neal explored other questions: What were the implications of that learning? In what ways could Elliott apply learning to other situations? What other learning would be helpful for Elliott? Once these questions were answered, Elliott focused on the process of learning, asking questions such as: What did we learn as a partnership? What did we learn as individuals about ourselves? How can we integrate that learning?

If the mentoring relationship has been beset with a problem, reaching a learning conclusion can be turned into a positive experience. In such a situation, mentoring partners should use the following approach:

1. Acknowledge the problem or difficulty encountered without casting blame or passing judgment—for example, "It looks as if we've come to an impasse."

2. If the decision is to end the mentoring relationship, make a clean break of it and end on an upbeat note. Consider what went right with the relationship as well as what went wrong—for example, "Let's look at the pluses and minuses of our relationship so that we can each learn something from the relationship."

3. Express mutual appreciation. Acknowledge the progress and accomplishments that did result from the relationship—for example, "Although we haven't been able to accomplish all of your objectives, we were successful in one area. I attribute our success to your persis-

tence and determination; those are the very characteristics you will need in your new job."

Celebrating Learning

We are more likely to celebrate success in our personal lives than in our workday life, where celebration is viewed as appropriate only within limits. In fact, celebration is a fundamental part of concluding a mentoring relationship because it reinforces learning and signals the transition process.

If celebration is to have any value, it must be genuine. When celebration is authentic, it engenders enthusiasm, builds a sense of community, and creates venues for communication. Terrence Deal and M. M. Key, in *Corporate Celebration: Play, Purpose and Profit at Work* (1998), speak to the value of celebrating: "Celebrations infuse life with passion and purpose. They summon the human purpose. They attach us to our human roots and help us soar toward new visions. They touch our hearts and fire our imaginations." (For more on celebration, see Kouzes and Posner, 1999.)

Mentoring relationships can be celebrated in a variety of settings, from formal events to informal meetings. Here are some specific suggestions for incorporating celebration into the closure of a mentoring relationship:

Collaborate on the planning. Engaging the mentee in the planning process will heighten the sense of individual contribution and foster the sense of partnership that permeates a mentoring relationship.

Elevate and expand knowledge. Use the celebration as a vehicle to continue to educate about the past, present, and future of the organization and use that as a context for growth. Ask your mentee to relate her or his perspectives, experiences, and challenges.

Leverage learning. The opportunity to leverage and maximize learning is the very essence of a mentoring relationship. By sharing your own development stories with your mentee, you create a sense of momentum that extends beyond the celebration.

Expand your thinking. When considering how to celebrate, look for permanent mementos or meaningful ways to remember the partnership.

Brag about accomplishments. Boast about your mentoring accomplishments with your mentee. Celebrate the triumphs and big wins triumphantly and with big celebrations. And while you are at it, make connections with the mentee's personal mission (and if you are mentoring in an organizational context, with the organization's mission).

Rekindle memory. Revisit the journey. There is an old saying, "If you don't have a sense of where you come from, going backward looks like progress." Look to create a shared sense of progress and purpose with your mentee. You may find that it will reawaken your own sense of purpose and keep the focus on learning.

Appreciate. Honor achievement. Let mentees know what it is that you appreciate about them. Tell them they matter and why (and be honest when you do). Leave space and opportunity for mentees to express their appreciation to you. This allows them to feel that they are giving something of themselves to you.

Talk about transitions. Talk about changes before they take place. Celebration is an opportunity to create self-awareness, educate for change, and prepare for next steps.

Espouse the vision. Articulating personal (and organizational) vision harnesses energy and engages the spirit. Linkages to vision help leverage learning. Create consistent thought and action by helping your mentee keep the vision out front.

Celebration is nurturing; it engages people through connection. It is the quintessential relationship-building opportunity. Challenge yourself and your mentee to create ways to celebrate. Celebrate the mini-miles, mile markers, and finish lines.

Deal and Key (1998) describe effective celebrations as "well-crafted processes that embrace and honor participants" (p. 207). And it was Kahlil Gibran (1964) who spoke so eloquently about the value of personalism in gift giving: "You give but little when you give of your possessions. It is when you give of yourself that you truly give" (p. 19). Personalism should be part of mentoring celebration. Exhibit 7.2 contains a list of ideas for celebration.

Coming to Closure About Closure

Good closure should elevate a mentee's learning and catapult it forward, raising the learning to another level. Unsatisfactory closure can block growth by minimizing the desire to achieve learning goals. Although individual need for closure varies, at least some closure is essential for growth. When mentoring partners do not come to closure, they sacrifice the potential for future learning.

The process of coming to closure is not just for the benefit of the mentee or the mentoring relationship. It presents a development opportunity for the mentor as well. After closure of the relationship, mentors should take

EXHIBIT 7.2

Ideas for Celebration

Gift Giving Opportunities

Gifts—a meaningful token or souvenir related to the purpose of the mentoring relationship—should be kept to a minimum and be modest in cost.

These might include:

- Books relating to a particular area of interest

- Inspirational and motivational books

- Blank journals for reflection and in preparation for the next mentoring journey

Written Expressions

Written notes offer a permanent record of support and encouragement as well as a memento. You might send a written note focusing on any of the following:

- What you learned from your mentee

- Something that has special meaning for you

- A good luck message

- Motivational messages for the future

Face-to-Face Conversations

Sometimes the right words uttered at just the right moment are the best and most remembered gifts in the long term. In expressing appreciation, be specific and focus on behaviors. It reminds the person of their value.

- "I admire your . . ."

- "You have a real knack for . . ."

- "I especially appreciated it when you . . ."

EXERCISE 7.2

Turning Closure into Learning: Mentor Self-Reflection

Instructions: Use the following sentence stems to reflect on what you have learned from your mentoring relationship.

1. What I have learned about myself . . .

2. My mentoring gifts and strengths . . .

3. What I wish I could learn to do better . . .

4. How I will apply what I have learned . . .

5. Specific steps for applying what I have learned . . .

EXERCISE 7.3

Coming to Closure: A Readiness Checklist

Instructions: Answer each of the questions, adding examples after each response. The first six questions by themselves provide a checklist for concluding the closure conversation.

____ Did we use the closure protocols we established to bring closure to the relationship effectively?

____ Did we hold a meaningful learning conclusion conversation?

____ Did we adequately evaluate learning outcomes?

____ Did we discuss the application and integration of new learning?

____ Were accomplishments acknowledged?

____ Were the milestones celebrated?

____ Was I able to identify the signals when it was time for closure?

____ Did I personally evaluate my own learning as a result of this experience?

____ Have I identified ways to apply and integrate my new learnings?

____ Have I decided what I would do differently as a mentor the next time?

time to focus on their own learning and consider how they can apply what they have learned to their advantage in future mentoring relationships. Exercise 7.2 provides a worksheet for mentor self-reflection.

The Aftermath

Even after the mentor and mentee have come to closure, there may be times when the mentee reappears in the mentor's life. It could be by way of a personal visit some years later, a letter, an e-mail, or a telephone call. At these mostly unpredictable times, the mentee will likely report on her accomplishments and wait for the mentor's approval. In this way, mentors become a bellwether in mentees' lives for measuring progress and receiving validation and kudos for their accomplishments. The aftermath exchange is a satisfying but very different exchange from the relationship that spawned the initial learning experience.

Less often, former mentees show up in a mentor's life and stay. Witness the experience that Mitch Albom describes in *Tuesdays with Morrie,* where a bond is rekindled and learning takes place at deeper and even more profound levels.

Moving On

Coming to closure in mentoring is an important part of learning, development, satisfaction, and promise. Closure links the present to the future for mentee and mentor.

Effective mentoring comes from learning throughout the mentoring relationship. A mentor's ability to learn from his or her mentee's own learning is an important development opportunity. To be sure it is time to move on, answer the questions in Exercise 7.3. If you cannot answer all the questions affirmatively, you may need to do more work on your own mentoring partnership to come to closure successfully. Refer to items 1 through 6 with your partner at the end of the closure conversation to make sure that you have covered all the necessary bases.

You may also find it helpful to revisit the ROS matrix in Exercise 3.1 and complete the rows in the fourth section.

CHAPTER 8

Regenerating Personal Growth Through Mentoring

According to *The Odyssey*, Mentor was entrusted with the education and development of Odysseus's young son, Telemachus. Mentor was the guardian who protected; he was wisdom personified and the dispenser of knowledge. He was the consummate teacher, who faithfully educated Telemachus in the ways of the world and gave him the requisite knowledge to live in that world. When Telemachus grew up and Odysseus returned, his responsibilities as mentor were complete.

"Mentoring has come a long way from its original purpose of enlightenment" (Landis, 1990, p. 28). Although the original concept of a mentor as a "loyal and trusted counsel" exists, it is woefully incomplete. Today's mentor is hardly the all-knowing source of wisdom that dispenses knowledge, hands out truths, and protects and guards. Rather, today's mentor is a facilitative partner in an evolving learning relationship focused on meeting mentee goals and objectives. Mentees are likely to have many mentors over the course of a lifetime, based on their individual needs at a specific point in time.

Today's mentor enjoys the benefits of rich learning opportunities that mentoring provides for mentors as well as mentees. A mentor's own growth and development are nurtured through reflection, renewal, and regeneration.

Bertrand, Marna, Leslie, and Elisha exemplify mentors who facilitate effective learning relationships. Their experiences describe positive learning outcomes that contributed to regenerating their own personal growth.

Bertrand, a retired interior designer, finds that mentoring reenergizes him. It adds to his sense of purpose, keeps him abreast of what is current in the furniture industry, and makes him feel useful. By mentoring young people, which he has done for the past seven years, he is always engaged in doing something new.

Marna holds a chair of distinction at her university. She is a well-known and respected scholar and has been mentoring students for three decades. Students flock to her classes just to be in her presence. One of the greatest joys and pleasures of her career is mentoring the next generation of scholars. She derives enormous personal satisfaction from sharing her expertise and experience. As her mentees begin their academic journeys and grow and then distinguish themselves in their careers, she keeps a watchful eye. Mentees continue to share insights with her for many years after their mentoring relationships have come to closure. These insights force her to reengage with concepts and ideas in new ways. Mentoring has prolonged and energized her six-decade career.

Leslie, a career counselor and pastor, looks forward to mentoring relationships because of the constant exposure to new ways of thinking, perspectives, and views it brings. What he learns from his mentoring relationships stimulates new ideas and pinpoints areas for his personal growth and development. He feels that he learns as much from his mentees as they learn from him.

Elisha, an attorney in a large law firm, has mentored many mentees, some more successfully than others. She attributes the development of her relationship skills to the feedback she has received from mentees. She takes their comments very seriously and has worked diligently to develop the interpersonal skills to which she attributes her career success.

Each of these mentors credits mentoring as having contributed to their personal growth and enrichment. They also manage (although it is not evident from the descriptions above) to build regular reflection into their mentoring.

Reflection

Critically reflective mentors find that they are more focused in their mentoring relationships. They bring expanded energy, take more informed action, and are generally more satisfied with their mentoring relationships. They also experience a carry-over to their personal and professional relationships as the habit of critical reflection becomes internalized.

Martha had been a mentor several times during her fifteen-year career as a public service employee. In one formal mentoring relationship, the focus was on orienting a new employee. In another, an informal mentoring relationship, she was mentoring a friend who was working on rebuilding her image. She also mentored a man who had moved to the United States from Argentina and wanted to set up a home-based business. She enjoyed each of these relationships and received a good deal of satisfaction from watching each of her mentees succeed.

Only recently, when she reflected on the quality of her mentoring interaction, did she realize that her previous relationships had been more about transfer of knowledge than self-directed learning. This was a real opening for her in terms of reflecting on who she was as a mentor and how she was able to enrich a mentoring relationship. As a result, she started reading about mentoring and learning all she could about the process. The more she read, the more she realized that mentoring was about her own growth and that reflection needed to become a regular part of her mentoring practice.

The Gifts of Renewal and Regeneration

Mentoring also provides an opportunity for renewal and regeneration. Being critically reflective throughout the phases of a mentoring relationship generates new insights about oneself, mentoring partners engaged in the relationship, and the learning relationship. One of the gifts of renewal is the sense of redefined purpose and energy that it brings.

Cyril was in a high-pressure job and always on the run, whether he was on the road or in the office. Still, he continued to connect regularly with his two mentees. He enjoyed the intellectual and emotional stimulation each provided, and therefore he made the relationships a priority. Cyril's mentoring experience ultimately reconnected him with his sense of purpose and made him rethink his priorities.

Mentoring offers the gift of regeneration too. First a mentor needs to be open to receiving the gift. When mentors do not take time to prepare adequately for the mentoring relationship and reflect on their learning, they are not growing and could be limiting the growth of their mentees. Sometimes the learning comes about serendipitously.

Prior to her mentoring relationship with Clark, Dana had had no interest in sports. Her mentee, Clark, was a sports enthusiast whose spirited descriptions about games and events were contagious. As a result, her curiosity was piqued, and she began to listen more closely to the conversations her coworkers were having about sports, to which she had previously turned a deaf ear. As Dana learned more, she began to make connections between sports metaphors and her work as a leader. She became a keen observer of the team process. Whenever Dana watched sports coaches at work, she learned skills that she could apply as a mentor. Dana began seeing ordinary things from a whole new perspective and was having fun in the process.

What It Is All About

Facilitating effective learning relationships requires mentor preparation and reflection throughout the mentoring process. Learning from experience is the key lever in facilitating learning.

The tools included in this book are designed to stimulate and guide reflective mentoring practice by helping mentors to prepare thoughtfully and develop and expand existing skill repertoires. *The Mentor's Guide* offers an opportunity to reflect on learning and the mentoring relationship.

Here are some final do's and don'ts for facilitating the learning of your mentee and simultaneously your own growth and development:

Heighten awareness. This book is a guide to facilitating effective mentoring relationships. Heightened awareness leads to more informed action. Use the concepts presented in this book to heighten your awareness. But do not be a slave to the forms and format.

Recapture the learning. This book advocates reflective practice. Capturing the action and taking time to learn from it as it happens empowers the mentor and facilitates the relationship. Take time after each relationship to recapture the learning. Do not wait until tomorrow; the advantage of being in the moment is lost.

Partner. This book presents partnership as a relationship of commitment and care that can be nurtured with the mentor's purposeful preparation. Partner with the learner. Do not let yourself become a dispenser of knowledge. Seek to promote self-directed learning.

Even when the soil has been tilled, the seeds planted, growth nurtured, and the harvest reaped, the journey is not over. Renewal and regeneration continue long after and provide unexpected delights. Perhaps the most treasured is the gift of growth.

The Gift of Growth

Marge Piercy's poem, "The Seven of Pentacles" (1982), which I have quoted from throughout the book, provides a compelling growth metaphor for the development of healthy mentoring relationships.

During the "growing season," as we engage in mentoring, we bring our own cycle, our own timetable, our own history, our own individuality, and our own ways of doing things. For learning to occur, we must understand what we bring and what our mentoring partner brings to the relationship. We must understand the complexity of the different components of the relationship. We must bring awareness of the learning process and an understanding of the ebb and flow of the mentoring phases. We must make connections, reaching out and drawing in so that mentoring is an enriching and satisfying experience.

What happens in a mentoring relationship can have a profound, deep, and enduring impact. The process of facilitating effective learning relationships through mentoring challenges each of us to think about what we might become.

APPENDIX A

Creating a Mentoring Culture

Organizations spend significant time and money developing mentoring programs. Some programs are successful for a limited period of time, while others continue to thrive and grow. The difference between the two lies in sustainability. Mentoring programs enjoy sustainability over time when mentoring is embedded in an organizational culture that values continuous learning.

This appendix, designed for program developers, administrators, and mentoring development teams, provides learning assistance for developing a mentoring process that will promote the emergence of a mentoring culture within an organization or other setting. It presents learning tools for addressing mentoring challenges (and the challenge of selecting a name for participant roles and program initiatives), ensuring that the necessary components are in place before a mentoring program begins, and a description of some of the indicators of a mentoring culture.

Addressing Mentoring Challenges

The development of a mentoring culture requires focus, discipline, and patience. Exhibit A.1 identifies common organizational mentoring challenges that must be thoughtfully considered and addressed in order to build the infrastructure necessary to nurture a mentoring culture. The questions and tasks involved in meeting each challenge can be helpful in focusing discussion and providing discipline for program developers, administrators, and mentoring development teams as they design and implement a viable mentoring process.

EXHIBIT A.1

Mentoring Design and Implementation Challenges

CHALLENGE 1: Define the purpose.

Questions:

- What are our business reasons for developing a mentoring program?
- What is the goal of the program?
- Whom will it serve?
- How will it benefit the participants?
- What learning outcomes should be realized as a result of participation?

Task:

Develop a clear, concise mission or purpose statement for the mentoring program.

CHALLENGE 2: Ensure visible support from top management.

Questions:

- What would support of top management look like?
- Who must be involved?
- How would they be involved?
- What would they be doing?
- Who are the current champions of the initiative?
- Who else has the potential to champion the effort?

Task:

Create an action plan for engaging top management in roll-out and support. Be specific and detail the necessary steps to make that happen.

CHALLENGE 3: Name the participants and the initiative.

Questions:

- What should the mentoring initiative be called? Program? Process?
- What should the participants be called? Mentors? Mentees? Protégés?

Task:

Decide on the names for participants and the mentoring initiative.

EXHIBIT A.1

Continued

CHALLENGE 4: Define mentee pool.

Questions:

- Who are the prospective mentees?
- What specific characteristics or needs should mentees have?
- What are the eligibility requirements?

Task:

Identify the target mentee population for mentoring program.

CHALLENGE 5: Create the mentor pool.

Questions:

- Who should serve as mentors? Who should not?
- What specific characteristics should mentors have?
- How will mentor candidates be recruited?
- How will they be selected?
- Will everyone who applies be accepted?
- What happens to mentor candidates who are not selected?
- What does it mean to be part of the mentor pool?
- How important is it to let people know they are in the pool?
- Should the pool be replenished? If so, how?

Task:

Identify procedures for creating and maintaining the mentor pool.

CHALLENGE 6: Identify roles and responsibilities.

Questions:

- What is the role of the mentor?
- What are the specific responsibilities?
- What is the role of the mentee?
- What are the specific responsibilities?
- What is the appropriate role of the manager or supervisor?
- Are there other "silent" partners affected or involved in the relationship?

EXHIBIT A.1

Continued

- What does mutual accountability mean?

- What should the duration of the relationship be?

- Should there be minimum and maximum time frames? If so, what should they be?

- Should we encourage flexibility regarding time frame?

- How many mentors or mentees should a person be engaged with at one time?

- Who has the responsibility to make the initial contact?

- What would regular interaction look like?

- Should training and education programming for mentors, mentees, and supervisors be required? Will it be voluntary?

Task:

Create a description of the roles and responsibilities for all parties involved in the mentoring relationship.

CHALLENGE 7: Develop pairing protocols.

Questions:

- How will mentees be identified?

- How will they be recruited?

- How will they be selected?

- What are the criteria for making matches?

- Will mentor matches be paired in advance?

- Who will make the matches? Will mentees select their own mentors?

- What is the next step once the match is made?

- What is the safety net if a match does not work out?

Task:

Create protocols for matching mentees and mentors.

CHALLENGE 8: Build a mentor education and training program.

Questions:

- What kind of training and education is needed?

- What is the knowledge to be transferred?

- Should we hold briefings, orientations, programs?

EXHIBIT A.1

Continued

- What kind of support is needed? (regular? occasional?)
- Should existing informal mentoring pairs be encouraged to participate in training and education programs?

Task:

Draft a training schedule. Identify the participants and the topics to be covered.

CHALLENGE 9: Identify ways to reward, recognize, and celebrate mentoring success.

Questions:

- How should mentoring be rewarded?
- Should all participants be recognized and rewarded?
- Should excellence in mentoring be recognized?
- How should accomplishments be celebrated?
- What would make an appropriate celebration?

Task:

Develop a reward, recognition, and celebration plan.

CHALLENGE 10: Define management, oversight, and coordination.

Questions:

- Who will establish policies and procedures for the program?
- What are our personnel needs?
- Who are the point persons?
- How should confidentiality and special circumstances be handled?
- What are the specific roles and responsibilities of the oversight committee?

Task:

Create a charge for the oversight team and job descriptions for the point persons.

EXHIBIT A.1

Continued

CHALLENGE 11: Identify methods and procedures for tracking progress and providing for continuous improvement.

Questions:

- What constitutes progress?
- How do we monitor the feedback process?
- How do we track numbers?
- How do we foster accountability?
- What are the criteria for measuring success?
- How do we measure success?
- Should we set targets for the next number of years? If yes, what might they be? (numbers? promotion?)

Task:

Define the criteria and determine the measurement and evaluation processes.

CHALLENGE 12: Plan the rollout.

Questions:

- What will full implementation look like?
- What would full rollout look like?
- What will the pilot program look like?
- How long will it take to put each piece in place?

Task:

Create specific time lines for rollout and a time line for full implementation.

CHALLENGE 13: Anticipate stumbling blocks and obstacles in the rollout process.

Questions:

- What obstacles might get in the way of a successful program rollout?
- What key issues is the organization dealing with over the next year that could affect the rollout or implementation of the mentoring program?
- Where will we face the greatest resistance?
- Who are the internal nay sayers?
- What false starts might we anticipate?
- What are the worst-case scenarios?

EXHIBIT A.1

Continued

Task:

Develop contingency plans for overcoming obstacles.

CHALLENGE 14: Plan the internal strategic communication campaign.

Questions:

- What have we learned from our stakeholder analysis?
- What key messages need to be communicated?
- Who needs to know what?
- What venues for communication are available?
- What is the time line for the internal communications plan?

Task:

Prepare a strategic communications plan.

CHALLENGE 15: Anticipate mentoring casualties (affecting individual mentoring relationships).

Questions:

- What kinds of mentoring casualties might occur?
- How would we define a mentoring casualty?
- What should be done about them?
- Who needs to be involved?

Task:

Identify specific policies and procedures for handling casualties.

Naming the participant roles and the mentoring initiative is a significant challenge that merits separate discussion. Considerable thought should be given to the names that are chosen when designing and implementing a mentoring program. Labels and names carry with them a wide range of meaning, explicit and implicit. In addition to the often hidden meaning, there is also a layer of historical or contextual meaning. "Most of the language of leadership is pitifully inadequate and that can turn off the very ambitious and mislead us all" (Sayles, 1990, p. 11).

Many names are used to describe the nonmentor partner in a mentoring relationship: mentee, mentoree, protégé, intern, learning leader, shadow, buddy, apprentice, peer mentor, co-learner, and others. The name should fit the purposes of the relationship. That is, the purposes of the mentoring relationship should be identified first and then the words used to designate that relationship.

Stepping Back

Once the challenges have been addressed and programmatic elements have been agreed on, it is beneficial to look at the mentoring process from a different perspective. The following tools provide a big-picture approach for analyzing the mentoring program design.

Readiness, Opportunity, and Support

Exercise A.1 is helpful for ensuring that key programmatic elements are in place. The answers to the questions about readiness focus on the identification of the key program elements that have been designed and are ready to be implemented, as well as those that are not yet complete. The outcome of the readiness discussion identifies elements that have been overlooked. Learning opportunities must exist on multiple levels in a mentoring culture in order to guarantee that diverse learning needs can be met. Support needs to be built in at every level of a mentoring program. There must be visible support for mentoring partners, mentee, mentor, and the individuals directly and indirectly affected by the relationship (the silent partners, such as supervisor or manager).

EXERCISE A.1

Applying the ROS Tool to Program Development

Instructions: This exercise can be completed as a group brainstorming activity addressing each element separately and then followed by group discussion. Or development team members can use this worksheet and complete it individually in advance of discussion. In either case, identify as many details as possible under each of the questions.

Element	Questions
Readiness	What programmatic elements are in place at this time? What elements are not yet in place? What is needed to get them in place?
Opportunity	What specific learning opportunities are available for program participants on an individual, partnership, and programmatic basis?
Support	What specific support has been built into the program?

Walk-Through

Simulation and role playing are two effective methods for realistically determining possible loopholes in the program. When you conduct the walk-through of the preliminary program design, it is instructive to work through the entire process using prototypes of typical program participants. Then candidly consider the questions about points of connection relating to the program and the relationship in Exercise A.2. The outcome of this exercise should also indicate if enough support has been built into the program infrastructure.

Addressing program development and implementation challenges and then stepping back to see the full picture increases the likelihood of creating a mentoring culture.

EXERCISE A.2

Program and Participant Points of Connection

Instructions: Completing each of the items below will help you to evaluate your walk-through.

Cracks and Loopholes

As you conduct a role play or simulated walk-through of the mentoring process you've designed, be aware of:

- Where someone might fall through the cracks in your program.

- What specific loopholes might yet need to be addressed.

Relationship Mapping

- Draw a clear map of the people involved in the mentoring relationship, including others in the workplace environment who have an impact on the behaviors of mentor and mentee. Examples include manager, supervisor, and subordinates.

- How might these relationships and connections need to link to the partners engaged in the relationship?

- How might these be misconstrued or compromise the primary mentoring relationship?

Indicators of a Mentoring Culture

Ten signs indicate that a mentoring culture has been created.

Accountability

Accountability is taken seriously. Everyone accepts accountability for maintaining the integrity of mentoring within the organization: mentoring partners, program coordinator, and oversight or advisory group. Benchmarking is routine, and improvement is a priority. Evaluation is an ongoing operating procedure, and results of surveys and progress are communicated throughout the organization.

Alignment

Mentoring is aligned within the culture, not an add-on to what is already in place. There are solid business reasons to engage in mentoring and adequate resources to support it. Mentoring is linked directly to corporate values that place high priority on individual and organizational learning.

Demand

The mentoring pool is brimming with people who are eager to become mentees and mentors. People want to participate in mentoring and seek out mentoring opportunities formally and informally. They request training, information, and resources. Some mentors and mentees are involved in simultaneous mentoring relationships.

Infrastructure

Resources, both human and financial, are in place in meaningful ways. The budget is ensured, and assigned individuals spend dedicated time on communication, training, mentor coaching, and administration. People are encouraged to respect and dedicate time for mentoring.

A Common Mentoring Vocabulary

People at different levels of the organization, from the water cooler to the boardroom, speak positively about mentoring. A shared vocabulary and set of assumptions informs conversations. People value mentoring experiences and seek out additional mentoring resources and learning opportunities.

Multiple Venues

Opportunities to engage in mentoring include, but are not limited to, group mentoring, long-distance mentoring, cross-cultural mentoring, one-on-one mentoring, mentoring circles, and mentoring networking. Resources are accessible and up-to-date.

Reward

Reward for mentoring is built into the culture. It may be part of a bonus system, it may be coded to meet hourly billing requirements, or there may be a stipend for participation. Reward may be tied to professional development goal achievement. There is acknowledgment and recognition for participation in different forums and formats.

Role Modeling

Best practices are the norm, and mentoring excellence is visible. Champions advocate for mentoring by being mentors themselves. Success stories are shared in public forums and communications.

Safety Net

Support is readily available to help, coach, and counsel mentors, mentees, mentoring partners, departments, and teams. Confidentiality is honored, and learning relationships that do not work out are assisted in reaching a positive learning outcome from mentoring experiences.

Training and Education

Training and education are strategically linked together as part of an overall plan to keep mentoring visible throughout the organization. Periodic briefings promote awareness by providing a common set of understandings about what mentoring means within the organizational framework. Skill building and renewal training for mentors and mentees are available as needed. The mentoring oversight group continuously educates itself on best practices. Organizations that lack in-house capacity make education and training outside the organization available.

APPENDIX B

Digging Deeper
Resources for Further Learning

As mentoring has become regarded as a business asset in the professions, industry, nonprofit organizations, government, and education, interest in the topic of mentoring continues to increase. Many authors approach the subject from a programmatic perspective and present best-practice models. Others use a more theoretical and conceptual perspective. Targeted handbooks and manuals for mentors, protégés and program administrators proliferate.

This appendix lists books that mentors might want to have on their bookshelf to assist in facilitating effective learning relationships. The parameters for selection were books that informed the development of *The Mentor's Guide*, give more in-depth treatment of the topics presented in this book, and complement one another to form a utilitarian, comprehensive, and balanced collection of resources.

Larry Daloz's *Mentor: Guiding the Journey of Adult Learning* is required reading for any mentor concerned with adult development and learning. Daloz uses the metaphor of the guide to describe the mentor's role in accompanying the learner on a journey. His depth perspective expands the current understanding of mentoring as a developmental journey. In addition, he offers rich examples and practical approaches to transform the learning and the learner.

Grounding the Work: Focusing on Learning

Belenky, M., Clinchy, B., Goldberger, N., and Tarule, J. *Women's Ways of Knowing: The Development of Self, Voice, and Mind*. New York: Basic Books, 1986.

> This book provides five approaches to understanding cognitive development based on qualitative research with women. The authors' findings about how individuals receive and process knowledge are applicable to both men and women. Connected knowing (in contrast to separate knowing) is congruent with the type of effective mentoring practice espoused in *The Mentor's Guide*. Knowledge about ways of knowing helps explain behavior and develop the mentor's ability to understand how mentees process knowledge.

Brookfield, S. D. *Understanding and Facilitating Adult Learning: A Comprehensive Analysis of Principles and Effective Practices*. San Francisco: Jossey-Bass, 1986.

> Effective facilitation is a basic process skill in the mentor's tool kit. The author presents an in-depth description of the facilitation process. Using six principles of effective practice, he outlines ways to keep the learning relationship on track in order to stimulate reflection and assist mentors in helping mentees reflect on their learning processes.

Candy, P. C. *Self-Direction for Lifelong Learning: A Comprehensive Guide to Theory and Practice*. San Francisco: Jossey-Bass, 1991.

> Mentors and mentees engage with the self-directed learning process at some level. Having an awareness of the theoretical framework that supports self-directed learning, both personally and for others, is imperative for mentors. Candy offers a process for critically reflecting on how learning can easily be applied in a mentoring relationship.

Cranton, P. *Understanding and Promoting Transformative Learning: A Guide for Educators of Adults*. San Francisco: Jossey-Bass, 1994.

> Mentors who foster learner empowerment, stimulate transformative learning, and support the learning process encourage mentee development. Having a personal theory of adult learning is invaluable in making decisions about the appropriate steps to encourage learning.

Galbraith, M. W. *Facilitating Adult Learning: A Transactional Process*. Malabar, Fla.: Krieger Publishing Company, 1991.

This book offers mentors multiple approaches for meeting different learning needs, expectations, value systems, and levels of ability of mentees. Among these approaches are using reflection on learning as a means to guide choices, individualizing the instructional process, using technology to enhance teaching and learning transactions, evaluating the learning process, and using counseling and helping skills to foster adult learning.

Merriam, S. B., and Caffarella, R. S. *Learning in Adulthood.* San Francisco: Jossey-Bass, 1991.

A key to mentoring excellence is understanding adult learners: how they learn best, their learning styles, how they develop over time, and the impact of aging on the ability to learn. Merriam and Caffarella offer theoretical and practical examples of the process, practical ways to locate supporting resources, and a discussion of the role of the learning facilitator.

Mezirow, J., and Associates. *Fostering Critical Reflection in Adulthood: A Guide to Transformative and Emancipatory Learning.* San Francisco: Jossey-Bass, 1990.

When mentoring partners are able to peel away the personal blinders and protective armor that have developed across time, they become open to the possibility for transformative learning. The process, which Mezirow and Associates describe, enables mentors to challenge assumptions and beliefs empathetically, as well as to create and facilitate developmental dialogue.

Tennant, M., and Pogson, P. *Learning and Change in the Adult Years: A Developmental Perspective.* San Francisco: Jossey-Bass, 1995.

Tennant and Pogson offer a psychology-based developmental perspective integrating adult teaching and learning. Their perspectives on adult development from a social, cultural, and historical point of view provide a challenging framework for guiding the learning process in a mentoring relationship.

Working the Ground: Considering Context

Kridel, C., Bullough, R., and Shaker, P. *Teachers and Mentors: Profiles of Distinguished Twentieth Century Professors of Education.* New York: Garland, 1996.

The most effective mentors know how to direct rather than dictate, to guide rather than smother; in other words, they know how to facilitate learning. This book is filled with stories by professors that illustrate the characteristics that allow mentors to do just that. Each relationship described presents a slightly different model for mentoring; each explores how the relationship formed and worked, and what both mentor and mentee gained.

Maack, M. N., and Passet, J. *Aspirations and Mentoring in an Academic Environment: Women Faculty in Library and Information Science.* Westport, Conn.: Greenwood Press, 1994.

Maack and Passet offer a full range of insights to mentors in an academic environment. Based on a cross-generational study of women in library and information sciences, the book includes implications for the practice of mentoring in general. Experiences are placed in the broader context of women's studies, sociology, psychology, management, anthropology, and higher education.

Megginson, D., and Clutterbuck, D. *Mentoring in Action: A Practical Guide for Managers.* London: Kogan Page, 1995.

This book will be of special interest to those involved in mentoring mentees challenged with overcoming disadvantage in career development and job displacement caused by race, gender, age, disability, or record of offending. It may be especially helpful for mentoring work that is based in Europe, although its application is not limited to mentors of the disadvantaged or to other than American settings.

Morrison, T., Conaway, W., and Borden, G. *Kiss, Bow, or Shake Hands.* Holbrook, Mass.: Bob Adams, 1994.

Knowledge about cultural customs helps avoid errors that can seriously damage mentoring relationships. This book provides knowledge about business practices, negotiation techniques, cognitive styles, and social customs for sixty countries. Each country is described in terms of history, religion, demographics, language, cultural orientation, business practices, and social protocols. Tips on gift giving, value systems, gestures, business entertaining, and more are included.

Murrell, A., Crosby, F., and Ely, R. *Mentoring Dilemmas: Developmental Relationships Within Multicultural Organizations.* Hillside, N.J.: Erlbaum, 1999.

As businesses and educational organizations become increasingly diversified, mentoring approaches must also reflect diversity. Shaped by conversations about dilemmas faced by mentors and mentees, Murrell, Crosby, and Ely demonstrate how theory and practice can be effectively integrated into a well-managed approach that meets diverse contextual needs.

Special Libraries Association. *Career Strategies: The Power of Mentoring.* Washington, D.C.: Special Libraries Association, 1990.

This collection focuses on establishing effective mentoring relationships in organizational contexts, including cross-cultural corporations. The mentor's role is described as teacher, tutor, colleague, and coach. Critical skills of mentors are discussed, including the ability to question, listen, and provide feedback. The book also includes tips for managing a relationship where the mentor is the mentee's supervisor.

Vella, J. *Learning to Listen, Learning to Teach: The Power of Dialogue in Educating Adults.* San Francisco: Jossey-Bass, 1994.

The mentor's teaching philosophy is key to ensuring the success of a mentoring partnership. This book increases understanding about meaningful dialogue between teacher and learner and how two-way communication strengthens the processes of adult learning. The examples that Vella offers will be particularly relevant to those engaged in a cross-cultural mentoring relationship.

Tilling the Soil: Preparing

Bell, C. R. *Managers as Mentors: Building Partnerships for Learning.* San Francisco: Berrett-Koehler, 1996.

Written for managers who have assumed responsibility for mentoring employees, Bell's book is full of techniques, strategies, and steps for building the careers of direct reports and making the role of mentor both comfortable and possible. Grounded in a partnership philosophy, the book will aid in understanding power-free facilitation of learning, consultation, and connected mentoring. It examines personal strengths as a mentor, how to give advice and feedback, and the importance of deep listening.

Kram, K. E. *Mentoring at Work: Developmental Relationships in Organizational Life.* Glenview, Ill.: Scott, Foresman, 1985.

This classic book provides a realistic view of the mentoring process based on years of research in corporate settings. The book focuses on the role of workplace mentoring relationships in promoting personal development during early, middle, and later career stages. It examines the potential benefits and limitations and illustrates various forms of development relationships through case studies and analysis.

Planting Seeds: Negotiating

Gilley, J. W., and Boughton, N. W. *Stop Managing, Start Coaching! How Performance Coaching Can Enhance Commitment and Improve Productivity.* Burr Ridge, Ill.: Irwin, 1996.

With recent changes in organizational configurations, managers often find their jobs reshaped and redefined. In the process, many become performance coaches who mentor, train, provide career counseling, and help employees use confrontation and conflict productively. An extensive chapter on mentoring frames the mentor's role as a guide in unlocking the mysteries of an organization. This self-help book will assist mentors in defining roles and relationships, particularly within a business environment.

Phillips-Jones, L. *The New Mentors and Protégés: How to Succeed with the New Mentoring Partnerships.* Grass Valley, Calif.: Coalition of Counseling Centers, 1993.

Phillips-Jones frames the primary role of the mentor as that of teacher; concepts of timing, pacing, and content of learning are addressed, as are interpersonal skills of both mentor and protégé. Potential problems with mentoring relationships and possible solutions are explored, such as excessive time and energy commitments, unrealistic or low expectations, mismatches, jealousy, and sexual involvement.

Nurturing Growth: Enabling

Bridges, W. *Transitions: Making Sense of Life's Changes.* Reading, Mass.: Addison-Wesley, 1980.

One might describe the entire mentoring relationship as a journey through transition. It is the transitions in life that bring adults to mentoring relationships. This book offers many insights into the transition process and concrete strategies and processes for making successful transitions, which mentors can use to guide mentees through the process of recognizing the new beginnings, making sense out of them, and learning from them.

Nichols, M. P. *The Lost Art of Listening.* New York: Guilford Press, 1995.

Communication is closely linked to learning in a mentoring relationship. This book provides insights into strengthening communication skills in building connections, particularly those as a listener. The insights offered in relation to the difference between real dialogue and simply taking turns at talking; hearing what people mean rather than simply what they say; dealing with defensiveness and differences of opinion; and understanding how the nature of a relationship affects listening are helpful in facilitating effective learning relationships.

Tannen, D. *You Just Don't Understand: Women and Men in Conversation.* New York: Ballantine Books, 1990.

Men and women may share a language, but how they use it and what it means reflect different approaches to relationships. Men typically anchor their identity in effective problem solving and action; women tend more toward a focus on the quality of relationships. Understanding and using gender differences respectfully promotes effective communication, the sine qua non of mentoring. Tannen's descriptions of gender-specific behaviors and language and the ways in which communication between men and women gets blocked offer helpful insights for mentoring.

Huang, C. A., and Lynch, J. *Mentoring: The Tao of Giving and Receiving Wisdom.* New York: HarperCollins, 1995.

Maintaining trust, compassion, and connection is foundational to an effective mentoring relationship. An underlying theme of this book is the centeredness that results when both partners have clarity of intent and like-mindedness of purpose. Centeredness is used to frame the mentor's various roles and suggest ways to provide meaningful communication and connection between the partners.

References

Albom, M. *Tuesdays with Morrie.* New York: Doubleday, 1997.

Alpine, L. "Learning to Reflect Using Journals as Professional Conversations." *Adult Learning,* Jan. 1992.

American Society for Training and Development Member Mailbag. *The Successful Global Trainer.* Alexandria, Va.: American Society for Training and Development, Aug. 1999.

Aubery, R., and Cohen, P. M. *Working Wisdom: Timeless Skills and Vanguard Strategies for Learning Organizations.* San Francisco: Jossey-Bass, 1995.

Bardwick, J. "Changing Culture." *Executive Excellence,* Aug. 1998, p. 10.

Bateson, M. C. *Composing a Life.* New York: Atlantic Monthly Press, 1989.

Belenky, M., Clinchy, B., Goldberger, N., and Tarule, J. *Women's Ways of Knowing: The Development of Self, Mind, and Voice.* New York: Basic Books, 1986.

Bell, C. R. *Managers as Mentors: Building Partnerships for Learning.* San Francisco: Berrett-Koehler, 1996.

Berends, P. B. *Coming to Life: Traveling the Spiritual Path in Everyday Life.* San Francisco: Harper San Francisco, 1990.

Bolman, L. G., and Deal, T. E. *Leading with Soul: An Uncommon Journey of Spirit.* San Francisco: Jossey-Bass, 1995.

Booher, D. "Need for Feedback." *Executive Excellence,* 1998, *15*(10), 4.

Bridges, W. *Transitions: Making Sense of Life's Changes.* Reading, Mass.: Addison-Wesley, 1980.

Brookfield, S. D. *Understanding and Facilitating Adult Learning.* San Francisco: Jossey-Bass, 1986.

Brookfield, S. D. *The Skillful Teacher: On Teaching, Trust, and Responsiveness in the Classroom.* San Francisco: Jossey-Bass, 1990.

Brookfield, S. D. *Becoming a Critically Reflective Teacher.* San Francisco: Jossey-Bass, 1995.

Candy, P. C. *Self-Direction for Lifelong Learning: A Comprehensive Guide to Theory and Practice.* San Francisco: Jossey-Bass, 1991.

Corey, E. R. Harvard Business School Case Study #9-581-058 (rev. 5/81), 1980.

Cranton, P. *Understanding and Promoting Transformative Learning: A Guide for Educators of Adults.* San Francisco: Jossey-Bass, 1994.

Cross, K. P. *Adults as Learners: Increasing Participation and Facilitating Learning.* San Francisco: Jossey-Bass, 1981.

Daloz, L. *Effective Teaching and Mentoring.* San Francisco: Jossey-Bass, 1986.

Daloz, L. *Mentor: Guiding the Journey of Adult Learners.* San Francisco: Jossey-Bass, 1999.

Deal, T. E., and Key, M. K. *Corporate Celebration: Play, Purpose and Profit at Work.* San Francisco: Berrett-Koehler, 1998.

DePree, M. *Leadership Is an Art.* New York: Doubleday, 1989.

Galbraith, M. W. *Facilitating Adult Learning: A Transactional Process.* Malabar, Fla.: Krieger Publishing Company, 1991.

Gibran, K. *The Prophet.* New York: Knopf, 1964.

Gilley, J. W., and Boughton, N. W. *Stop Managing, Start Coaching! How Performance Coaching Can Enhance Commitment and Improve Productivity.* Burr Ridge, Ill.: Irwin, 1995.

Goleman, D. "What Makes a Leader?" *Harvard Business Review,* 1998, 76(6).

Havighurst, R. J. *Development Tasks and Education.* New York: McKay, 1961.

Helgeson, S. *The Web of Inclusion.* New York: Doubleday, 1995.

Huang, C. A., and Lynch, J. *Mentoring: The Tao of Giving and Receiving Wisdom.* San Francisco: Harper San Francisco, 1995.

Knowles, M. S. *The Modern Practice of Adult Education: From Pedagogy to Andragogy.* River Grove, Ill.: Follett.

Kolb, D. *Experiential Learning: Experience as the Source of Learning and Development.* Upper Saddle River, N.J.: Prentice Hall, 1984.

Kouzes, J.. M., and Posner, B. Z. *Encouraging the Heart: A Leader's Guide to Rewarding and Recognizing Others.* San Francisco: Jossey-Bass, 1999.

Kram, K. E. *Mentoring at Work: Developmental Relationships in Organizational Life.* Glenview, Ill.: Scott, 1988.

Kridel, C., Bullough, R., and Shaker, P. *Teachers and Mentors: Profiles of Distinguished Twentieth Century Professors of Education.* New York: Garland, 1996.

Krupp, J. A. "Self-Renewal, Personal Development and Change." *Adult Learning,* 1995, 6.

Landis, M. C. "Mentoring as a Professional Development Tool." *Continuing Higher Education,* Winter 1990.

Lencioni, P. *The Five Temptations of a CEO: A Leadership Fable.* San Francisco: Jossey-Bass, 1998.

Lewis, L., and Dowling, L. "Making Meaning and Reflective Practice." *Adult Learning,* 1992, *3*(4).

Lindeman, E. C. *The Meaning of Adult Education.* Norman: Printing Services, University of Oklahoma, 1989.

Lindenberger, J. and Zachary, L. J. "Using 20/20 to Develop a Successful Mentoring Program: Lessons From the Field." *Training and Development,* Feb. 1999.

Loder, J. E. *The Transforming Moment.* (2nd ed.) Colorado Springs, Colo.: Helmers & Howard, 1989.

Maack, M. N., & Passet, J. *Aspirations and Mentoring in an Academic Environment: Women Faculty in Library and Information Science.* Westport, Conn.: Greenwood Press, 1994.

Megginson, D., and Clutterbuck, D. *Mentoring in Action: A Practical Guide for Managers.* London: Kogan Page, 1995.

Merriam, S. B., and Caffarella, R. S. *Learning in Adulthood.* San Francisco: Jossey-Bass, 1991.

Mezirow, J. "Perspective Transformation." *Adult Education,* Feb. 1978.

Mezirow, J., and Associates. *Fostering Critical Reflection in Adulthood: A Guide to Transformative and Emancipatory Learning.* San Francisco: Jossey-Bass, 1990.

Missirian, A. K. *The Corporate Connection: Why Executive Women Need Mentors to Reach the Top.* Upper Saddle River, N.J.: Prentice Hall, 1982.

Morrison, T., Conaway, W. A., and Borden, G. A. *Kiss, Bow or Shake Hands.* Holbrook, Mass.: Bob Adams, 1994.

Murray, M. *Beyond the Myths and Magic of Mentoring: How to Facilitate an Effective Mentoring Program.* San Francisco: Jossey-Bass, 1991.

Murrell, A., Crosby, F., and Ely, R. *Mentoring Dilemmas: Developmental Relationships Within Multicultural Organizations.* Hillside, N.J.: Erlbaum, 1999.

Neugarten, B. L. "Adult Personality: Toward a Psychology of the Life Cycle." In B. L. Neugarten (ed.), *Middle Age and Aging.* Chicago: University of Chicago Press, 1968.

Nichols, M. P. *The Lost Art of Listening: How Learning to Listen Can Improve Relationships.* New York: Guilford Press. 1995.

Owen, H. *Open Space Technology: A User's Guide.* Potomac, Md.: Abbott Publishing, 1992.

Phillips-Jones, L. *Mentors and Protégés: How to Establish, Strengthen and Get the Most from a Mentor-Protégé Relationship.* New York: Arbor House, 1982.

Phillips-Jones, L. *The New Mentors and Protégés.* Cypress Valley, Calif.: Coalition of Counseling Centers, 1997.

Piercy, M. *Circles on the Water.* New York: Knopf, 1982.

Prichett, P., and Pound, R. *The Stress of Organizational Change.* Dallas, Tex.: Prichett & Associates, 1995.

Progoff, I. *At a Journal Workshop.* New York: Dialogue House, 1975.

Quinn, R. E. *Deep Change: Discovering the Leader Within.* San Francisco: Jossey-Bass, 1996.

Rogers, M. E. *A Generational Xchange: A Guide to Managing and Mentoring Generation X.* New York: Deloitte & Touche and the Corporate State, 1999.

Rose A. "Framing Our Experience." *Adult Learning,* 1992, *3*(4).

Sayles, L. R. "Leadership for the Nineties: Challenge and Change." *Issues and Observations,* Spring 1990, *10*(2).

Schlossberg, W. K., Lynch, A. Q., and Chickering, A. W. *Improving Higher Education Environments for Adults.* San Francisco: Jossey-Bass, 1989.

Schön, D. *The Reflective Practitioner.* New York: Basic Books, 1983.

Shea, G. *Mentoring: Helping Employees Reach Their Full Potential.* New York: AMA-COM, 1994.

Special Libraries Association. *Career Strategies: The Power of Mentoring.* Washington, D.C.: Special Libraries Association, 1990.

Smith, H. W. *The 10 Natural Laws of Successful Time and Life Management: Proven Strategies for Increased Productivity and Inner Peace.* New York: Warner Books, 1995.

Tannen, D. *You Just Don't Understand: Women and Men in Conversation.* New York: Ballantine Books, 1990.

Tennant, M., and Pogson, P. *Learning and Change in the Adult Years: A Developmental Perspective.* San Francisco: Jossey-Bass, 1995.

Vella, J. *Learning to Listen, Learning to Teach: The Power of Dialogue in Educating Adults.* San Francisco: Jossey-Bass, 1994.

Zachary, L. J. "Mentoring Relationships: Using Partner Preparation Tools." *Mentor,* 1994a, *6*(4).

Zachary, L. J. "Mentoring Relationships: Self-Directed Preparation Strategies." *Mentor,* 1994b, *6*(1).

Zachary, L. J. "Mentoring Relationships: Coming to Closure." *Mentor and Protégé,* 1997, *9*(4).

Zachary, L. J. "Creating a Mentoring Culture." *All About Mentoring,* 1997, no. 11.

Index